RESEARCH WRITING

ABOUT CULTURAL ARTIFACTS

Anna Faktorovich

ANAPHORA LITERARY PRESS

QUANAH, TEXAS

ANAPHORA LITERARY PRESS
1108 W 3rd Street
Quanah, TX 79252
https://anaphoraliterary.com

Book design by Anna Faktorovich, Ph.D.

Printed in the United States of America, United Kingdom and in Australia on acid-free paper.

Edited by: Margaret Blatz

Published in 2018 by Anaphora Literary Press

Research Writing About Cultural Artifacts
Anna Faktorovich—1st edition.

Library of Congress Control Number: 2018906914

Library Cataloging Information
Faktorovich, Anna, 1981-, author.
    Research writing about cultural artifacts / Anna Faktorovich
    104 p. ; 9 in.
    ISBN 978-1-68114-436-8 (softcover : alk. paper)
    ISBN 978-1-68114-437-5 (hardcover : alk. paper)
    ISBN 978-1-68114-438-2 (e-book)
1. Language Arts & Disciplines—Composition & Creative Writing—General.
2. Reference—Research.
3. Reference—Writing Skills.
PE1001-1693: Modern English
306: Culture & institutions

RESEARCH WRITING

ABOUT CULTURAL ARTIFACTS

ANNA FAKTOROVICH

CONTENTS

Introduction   6
Part 1: Short Review Essays   8
Music Video Review Assignment
Concepts Involved in a Review
Summary
Close Reading
Proper Citations of Music Videos
Critical Research into a Single Source
Your Feelings versus Detached Analysis
How to Incorporate Theoretical Concepts
A Sea of Opinions and How to Shape and Defend Your Own
How to Avoid Unclear Writing

Part 2: Argumentative Essays   19
Class, Ideology and Power Assignment
Internet and Library Research Methods
    Searching for Sources at the Library: Technical Guide
    Research Philosophy
    Internet Information Overload
    Readings from the Library
Class, Ideology and Power Concepts

Part 3: Supporting Claims and Anticipating Objections   31
Logical Point of View
Logical Fallacies
Supporting Claims
Introduction Types
Anticipating Objections and Conflicting Points of View

Part 4: Clarity in Writing Style   41
Clichés
Empty Abstractions
Comprehension of Terms
Contextualization
Vagueness
Transitions

Part 5: The Rhetorical Form of a Research Essay   48
Genre
Modes of Discourse
Organization
Gender Bias Essay Assignment

Part 6: Formatting and Writing Essays on a Computer   60
Double-Spacing versus Single-Spacing
Paragraph Indentation
Fonts
Italics, Quotations, Bold or Underlines
Charts
Pictures
Tables
Inserting Automatic Parts
Footers
Symbols
Thesaurus
Track Changes
Group Writing Assignment
Ethnicity Essay Assignment

Part 7: Elements of Research   74
MLA Book and Part of a Book Citations
     Books
     Parts of Books
In-Text Citations
Plagiarism and Academic Integrity
Synthesis of Multiple Sources of Information

Part 8: The Research Paper   87
Research Paper Assignment
Strategies for Idea Invention
Narrowing the Topic
Organizing a Research Paper
Writing Exercise

Part 9: Grabbing Attention   98
Introductions and Conclusions

Introduction

Research writing courses in colleges across the world have a tendency to be dull, and similar to each other. They typically review the elements of the research paper and ask students to draft formulaic papers that fit the set guidelines. There have been plenty of textbooks written for these classes that repeat nearly identical information. This market is definitely over-saturated. On the other hand, a few universities in the United States and elsewhere are starting to teach classes like the Writing Cultural Studies class I taught at the University of Texas at Rio Grande Valley (UTRGV) in the 2016-7 academic year. UTRGV has set the goal of becoming bilingual and bicultural in a climate that is very hostile to the migration of Mexicans into America. UTRGV stands on the very border that is currently being walled off. In line with their mission to become culturally dualistic, UTRGV has started offering a Research Writing class that focuses on audio-visual entertainment (such as film or music) and other cultural artifacts, as well as diversity-related topics. This class offers more engaging topics for research than the repeating political or social topics that fit the formula of a traditional college research writing class. Students are likely to be more interested in researching films they watch for fun than dusty topics they are not personally invested in. More colleges are likely to start teaching these types of classes especially with help from textbooks like this one that suits this curriculum.

A search on Amazon and WorldCat does not turn up a single textbook that combines Cultural Studies with an introductory or advanced college writing course. There are plenty of books on the various individual branches of cultural studies, including gender or ethnicity studies. The book that comes closest to this is *Writing Against the Curriculum: Anti-Disciplinarily in the Writing and Cultural Studies Classroom*. This 2010 book includes several essays from professors who have taught cultural studies, and they offer unique advice on how writing can be taught in cultural studies classes. However, this idea is different from a Research Writing class that focuses on Cultural Studies. *Writing Against* is for advanced students of cultural studies rather than for the larger marketplace of students taking introductory composition classes. Other existing books look at travel writing through the lens of cultural studies, or offer collections of essays on cultural studies topics in different regions of the world. Thus, there is a clear demand for a textbook that would shake up the Research Writing curriculum. American students are reading less, and watching media more, a class that accepts this shift can embrace the students' preferences, stimulating their imagination and desire to learn.

This textbook combines the rigor of a Research Writing class with the imaginative and culturally significant realm of Cultural Studies. Concepts that are typically discussed in Research Writing textbooks, like close reading, thesis statement, and clichés, are covered in full. Complex rhetorical concepts are explained simply and fully. Additionally, the elements of a proper argument are not only digested for students, but are also assisted with discussions of political, economic, social and other types of cultural concepts such as communism or feminism. Teachers who are looking for ideas to inspire their plans, will find assignments across the book to utilize. This book is deliberately short and meant to be a cheap paperback, so that it can be utilized as a quick reference guide and idea book for cultural studies related topics (if not as the primary textbook for a course that entirely combines Research Writing with Cultural Studies).

Part 1

Short Review Essays

The first part of this book focuses on concepts related to researching and writing a music video review essay. I started these Writing Cultural Studies classes with this lighter assignment so that students can relax a bit as they take in some of the information they will need for later more intensive research projects. Every review has to achieve a succinct and relevant summary of the music video, so that readers who do not have a chance to view the video can feel as if they have seen it. There is also an explanation of what "close reading" implies. Unlike regular reading, a close reading finds clues in any cultural artifact including a pop music video. "How should a music video be cited?" students always ask before they write their first paper. This and many other practical questions about citation methods and other topics are answered. Researching a single video might seem like an easy task, but this type of analysis calls for very narrow research, so this process is closely explained. Because I've observed that students tend to react emotionally to their favorite videos, I included a section on "feelings versus detached analysis," where I explained why analysis is superior and how to perform it. The next section explains how to incorporate theoretical concepts into an essay that otherwise might rely on opinions students have about the video. They are also instructed on how to defend a narrow opinion, and how to write clearly.

Music Video Review Assignment

Write a 2-page or 5-paragraph Review Essay on your favorite or most disliked music video. You can write it on the video you chose for the 1-2 paragraph assignment or focus on a different video. If you focus on the same video, the content should be mostly new, rather than an edited version of the earlier review. If you only wrote a paragraph, you can use most of it in the longer review, but this especially applies to those who already wrote a 5-paragraph essay. Your work will be flagged for plagiarism by SafeAssign if you repeat the same content. Do not write more than 5 paragraphs or 2 pages. Your essay must include:

1. A description of the narrative depicted in the music video.
2. An explanation of the central theme in the video.
3. Your position and supporting evidence regarding if the video is primarily formulaic or innovative.
4. Use of one of the cultural studies terms we covered in the first week of class to explain the deeper significance or meaning behind the video.
5. Your argument and supporting evidence regarding if the video made a positive or a negative impression on you and why this was the case.
6. A Thesis Statement that summarizes your positive or negative position on the music video being reviewed.

This essay must be clearly written, and closely proofread. Grammatical mistakes stand in the way of clarity, so an excess of them will lower your grade. With this essay, you should demonstrate your understanding of the citation, writing, criticism and research methods that were explained in the lectures and course materials.

Concepts Involved in a Review

Summary

As I was grading your short responses to your favorite music video, I made several comments to individual students, which can also help many of the other students understand the assignment better. Read these guidelines carefully, as they are the equivalent of a chapter in a textbook you have to read to prepare for class. When I grade your essays, I will base my grades on your comprehension of these ideas.

Close Reading

If the first assignment asked you to write about a work of literature, it would have asked you to closely read the text. Instead, we are closely examining a musical video. But, you should use the same techniques you would have used if we were examining a book. Everybody that glances at a music video has some ideas about it running through their mind. The goal in this class is for you to learn how to think critically about all types of cultural artifacts. Critical thinking and evaluation means looking beyond surface impressions and to the cultural significance or meaning of the images, sounds or other sensory impressions. We discussed concepts such as "gender bias" and "aesthetics" last week. These are not just ideas or theories we touched on, but should be utilized as the basis on your criticism in Essay 1. Is a woman in the video objectified? Is there a political or economic ideology that the musician is supporting? When you think about an artifact in these terms, you are critically evaluating it with detached logic.

Proper Citations of Music Videos

Another common mistake was the lack of proper citations in your short review. For the first few essays, you will only be examining a single primary source. A **primary source** is an original artifact (book, diary, music video or the like) that can be examined for evidence it offers in support of your chosen argument. This class is focused on research writing. The most important component of research writing is proper citation of the sources utilized. Failure to properly cite a source can lead to charges of plagiarism in the extreme, or a lower grade on an assignment.

When you are only citing one source, in **casual writing** assignments, a hyperlink to the source and citing the title and the creator's name can be sufficient.

The **title** of the artifact should have all of the main first letters capitalized. The title of a short work, such as a music video, should also be in quotation marks. Longer works, such as a feature film, should be italicized. Minor words in the title should *not* be capitalized. YouTube and many other popular sources frequently automatically capitalize all of the words in a title. For example, the title for Taylor Swift's video might be written as, "Out Of The Woods." This is incorrect. The preposition, "of," and the article "the" are minor words in the phrase, and they should not be capitalized. Thus, the title should be written as, "Out of the Woods."

In a **formal essay** assignment or when you are writing for publication, to be on the safe side, you should include a full citation. We will primarily be using MLA citations in this class, but you should always ask regarding the best citation style as the Chicago and ALA citations are also popular in academia and in research fields. The requirements for newspaper or magazine articles are less formal than in research settings. The main difference is that you do not have to include parenthetical citations with the exact minute or page in the artifact you are reviewing where you found the bit of evidence you are quoting in a newspaper article. We will cover parenthetical citations later in the class. If you cite from more than one source in your papers before that point, you are responsible for looking up online or in the *MLA Handbook* how to properly cite multiple sources within the text. Even without the need to include in-text references, you still have to place all of the text that is a direct quote from the music video or another cultural artifact you are examining. If you are only examining one short music video, it should be easy for a reader to find the bits you are quoting from by watching the entire video. If you are criticizing a longer film or any written text, you have to give the minutes the text comes from or the pages you are citing even if you only use a single source. Try to think about these citations from the perspective of a fellow student that wants to contradict your findings and needs to find the context around the sentence(s) or phrase(s) you are quoting from.

Here is how a **quote from a music video** should look like:

Taylor Swift's music video, "Out of the Woods," begins with her singing, "Looking at it now…" This signifies that she is looking back at a past experience from a distant perspective in time.

There are a few points to pay attention to here. First, if you take a fragment out of a song, rather than an entire sentence, you should add an ellipse, as shown, which indicates that you left the quote in its midst. Second, if the quote starts at the beginning of a sentence, you should capitalize the first letter within the quote. Third, you have to insert a comma or a colon before a quote in parenthesis that follows your own words. Fourth, the spacing between quotation marks and the commas, and text around it should be as shown. Refer back to this example to avoid common mistakes of placing spaces where they should not go, or vice versa.

In formal essays, even if you only have a single source, it is a good idea to include a **"Works Cited"** section with the **details about the source**, as in:

Works Cited

Swift, Taylor. "Out of the Woods." Online video clip. *YouTube*. TaylorSwiftVEVO, 31 December 2015. Web. 5 September 2016.

The format used above is:

Author's Last Name, First Name. "Title of the Music Video." Online video clip. *Website's Name*. Name of Publisher, Date Published. Web. Date Retrieved.

Some of the items in the above citation, such as the line, "Online video clip," are optional, but this is a full citation that meets the most stringent requirements. The order of where the day of the month goes in relation to the name of the month, and various other elements in this formula are regulated by the citation style you are using, such as MLA or Chicago.

Critical Research into a Single Source

Even if you are evaluating a single music video, you still have to utilize critical research methods. The act of taking **direct quotes** from a primary source is one of the most common critical research components. However, if you take out a quote, and then fail to explain its relevance to your argument, you are not properly utilizing this resource. Any quote you take out should be used to prove your central Thesis or your Supporting Arguments. If you are criticizing a short music video, taking out phrases or a sentence is better than quoting an entire stanza. You are looking for things that pertain to the focus you are taking on the criticism. For example, if you are looking into gender bias in a video or lyrics, you should quote segments that objectify women, as opposed to also quoting parts that talk about material possessions. The narrower your focus is, the stronger your argument will be, as you will be able to offer more evidence to support it.

Narrating the story depicted in a music video is also a critical research method. You have to summarize what happened in the video in order to explain what it signifies. Think about a good narration as a story you would tell to a friend when trying to explain what happened in a great music video you saw. Better yet, try to imagine that you are explaining the narrative to somebody who is blind and deaf and has to rely on a brail transcript of your narration to obtain the full experience of the video. They did not hear the lyrics. They did not see how people were dancing, or what they were doing. At the same time, the point of this narration is not simply to summarize, but to focus on the elements that you are stressing in this particular argumentative essay. The narration should assist anybody that has never seen the video you are referring to before. It should help to further shape your central argument by providing some proof of gender bias, aesthetics, or another crucial element to your particular cultural artifact.

To explain if the video is formulaic or innovative, you will also have to bring in examples of other music videos that might have been similar in genre, style, theme, or other aspects to yours. **Comparing** (explaining the similarities) and **contrasting** (explaining the differences) are two helpful research methods that are essential to this part of the assignment. If you are summarizing the narrative or explaining other elements from additional sources, you do not have to create a full citation for them. You do have to give the name of the video and the name of its creator because this helps ground your arguments in sound research. Somebody that wants to double-check your opinions can find the videos you are referring to online and view them. Avoid making a general comparison such as the following attempt:

"Out of the Woods" is similar to so many other videos I've seen that all include a girl running from her problems.

The reader wants you to name specific examples of videos where a girl is running from her problems so that they can better understand your argument. You have to briefly summarize what happens in each of the similar videos in a phrase or sentence. As in this example:

> There have been several music videos in different genres that focused on a man or woman running from their problems. One example is Snoop Lion's "Tired of Running," where he raps that he is tired of running from the police, as he attempts to explain to his friends that he does not want to engage with them in the next shady business venture. Another example is Beyonce's "Naughty Boy—Running," which depicts a man running at the bottom of the ocean after becoming frightened by something in his life. Finally, Kip Moore's "Running for You" offers a different take on this idea as the protagonist is running after the woman he loves while she is moving away from him in their relationship.

I found these three examples by **searching** for "girl running music video" on YouTube. If you are having difficulty recalling the similar or contrasting videos you have seen before, you might also want to perform a similar search using the words that are central to your argument.

Similarly to searching for videos that match your argument, you should perform basic research when you run into word choice or other grammatical problems. If you are unsure about the definition of a word, **check a dictionary**, such as Dictionary.com. You can also look up synonyms for the word you are trying to use in Word via the "Thesaurus" tool under the Review tab. For example, if you search for the word "unsure" with this tool, the words that come up as its synonyms are "hesitant" or "doubtful," and its antonym is "sure." This gives you a general idea on if the word you plan on using is in the ballpark of your intended meaning or if it might say the opposite to or something other than what you were trying to write. Some words gain a different meaning when they are placed in the wrong context. I will usually comment that you have "word choice" problems when I see a few of these glitches. If you research the meanings of the words you are not as familiar with, you can avoid this awkward problem.

Your Feelings versus Detached Analysis

Your feelings are important, but if they dominate your critical writing, you are merely creating bad criticism. There is a difference between feelings and opinions. Your feelings might be that you felt loved, warm and fuzzy, or super-duper happy as you were watching the video. If you imagine that you are reading your essay to a deaf and blind person that desperately wants to visualize your argument, these general feelings offer little in the way of understandable proof. What does super-duper happy look like? What does it sound like? Why did a girl running from wolves make you so happy? When you talk about your feelings, think about them as the tone behind the music video. Does the video have an uplifting and positive message or is it glum and pessimistic? These distinctions can help you to critically evaluate the video. For example, if there is a depiction of objectification of women, you have to ask if the tone around this objectification is positive or negative. If the women are happy to be objectified, and the protagonists are delighted to make them into objects, there is a cultural problem with gender bias in the video. On the other hand, if the tone is dark and pessimistic, it is likely that the musician is criticizing objectification or is standing up against abuse of women. Step aside from being emotionally involved in the artifact and attempt to criticize it from an authoritative position. It is your job to explain what it is, and to offer an argument regarding what it represents. Only refer to your feelings if they are significant to defending your logical argument.

Narration is not enough for a critical review, your opinions and interpretations are essential. Do not simply point out that others have had an opinion about an artifact. You have to explain if you agree or disagree with earlier opinions (if you bring these in) and offer evidence from the artifact in support of your position. Opinions are central to a critical review, but do not let your emotions govern your opinions.

How to Incorporate Theoretical Concepts

There were some examples offered above of how a concept such as gender bias can be incorporated into an essay. This topic touches on various other fields covered by feminist or gender studies. Some people major in these fields or receive graduate degrees in them, so there is a lot to say on each of the concepts I went over in the first week. Without too much research, you should be able to criticize a music video in terms of objectification of the men or women in it. Discrimination against women and minorities is a common problem in American mainstream culture and you have probably frequently heard these terms used. This assignment is asking you to look beyond the surface and to the roots of this or another concept as it pertains to the artifact you are studying. A **theory** is a system of concepts and principles that jointly explain an element being studied. **Concepts** are abstract ideas, and in this context, they are abstract ideas about cultural artifacts. The narrative states the facts regarding what happened in the video. On the other hand, the concepts behind this surface storyline touch on more nebulous or theoretical ideas that expand a single video into an artifact that is significant to the understanding of the culture it is a part of.

A Sea of Opinions and How to Shape and Defend Your Own

If a music video is closely examined in a physical classroom, it is likely that students who write about the video following this discussion will echo the ideas that their fellow students stressed. On the other hand, if students think about the same video in isolation, it is more likely that they will have very different opinions about what it means. Studies have shown that witnesses to a crime frequently relate a very different narrative of what happened and what the suspect looked like. So, people also typically give diverging narrations of what happened in the same music video, if they see it in isolation. When the study of concepts or abstract ideas is added into this mix, there are countless quantities of interpretations of the same cultural artifact. This is wonderful news because it is likely that your opinions will differ from most other opinions, and so your research will be **original**. At the same time, you should try to think about what other people perceived in the same clip. It will be easier for you to make a strong argument if you are arguing against what you imagine somebody on the other side of the debate might write. For example, you might dislike all sappy love songs, and in your criticism you want to say this. If you imagine what somebody that enjoys sappy love songs might write in support of them, you can offer more precise arguments that knock down their flawed notions. **Both opinions can be defended** with evidence and logic. It is your job to win the argument, even if the opposing position will not be voiced in your review.

How to Avoid Unclear Writing

Later in this class, we will do some workshops in which you will read your fellow students' work and will offer comments about it. You probably have read unpolished work by your fellow students in the past. The biggest problem with reading such work is the difficulty one encounters with grasping the intended meaning. During the period between 1150 and 1500 (and before this point), grammatical and spelling rules were a lot looser than they are today and these variations is one of the reasons it is so difficult to read Middle English texts. *The Canterbury Tales* is one well known example from this period. The first part of the first story, "The Knight's Tale," begins with this line: "Heere bigynneth the Knyghtes Tale" (http://www.librarius.com/cantales.htm). If you read the entire book in Middle English, you might notice other variations on the spelling of "begins." And if you read other authors, they too offer other possibilities. Reading became more popular after the English language became more standardized with the help of books such as Samuel Johnson's *Dictionary of the English Language* (1755). If we all use the same grammatical rules and the same spellings, it is easier to interpret what various authors are attempting to communicate.

You obviously know what you are trying to say, but frequently after we put sketches of ideas down, they fail to capture our exact meaning. If you re-read what you wrote, you are taking a crucial step in catching mistakes that would confuse somebody else who is trying to read your work.

A common problem is leaving a sentence unfinished and attaching a second unfinished sentence to it. You might have many ideas at the same time, and the only way to keep them from running into each other is to re-read and proofread your work. If you re-read a **run-on set of sentences**, you will easily spot that you failed to finish the first idea before running on to the next.

Another common mistake is confusing plural and singular endings in verb and noun combinations. The verb and the noun should agree, or they should either both be singular or plural when they are connected to each other. You should be familiar with the rules of **verb and noun agreement**, and if you are not, you should read up about this problem to avoid it in the future.

Another problem to watch out for is introducing a new idea at the end of an argumentative essay without defending it. Even if I am not asking you to follow a strict five-paragraph order, you have to have a **beginning, middle and end** to all of your essays. At the end, you have to summarize your argument or re-state your Thesis. Your essay will be stronger if you delete the last-minute idea you have, and spend that bit of time on proofreading the content that is related to your central argument.

Do your best to **avoid going in circles** in your argument. You can repeat the central point in the title and the thesis, but avoid spending an entire essay on repeating your thesis without providing any proof. Too many writers enter the death-spiral of repeating variations of the same concept without so much as narrating the story portrayed or offering any logical arguments in support of this abstract idea. The assignment specifies that you have to narrate, criticize and perform other components, and if you keep repeating yourself, you will not succeed in fulfilling the key requirements. There is a limited amount of words you can include in a two-page essay, so you have to utilize each of them in a way that contributes to the mission of writing a well-researched essay.

Meanwhile, I noticed that many of you are having technical difficulties **with submitting your essays via Blackboard**. Attach essays as Word documents, instead of typing them in the comments section or attaching them as PDFs. I can comment over the text, or edit the text in Word documents, and I cannot do this in other types of submissions. In addition, when you write an essay in Word, it auto-corrects some common grammatical and spelling problems and underlines with a wiggly line grammatical and spelling issues you should research. Many punctuation mistakes are spotted by Word. You are unlikely to leave a blank space before the period at the end of a sentence with Word's help. PDFs and other file types might not be picked up as readable by Blackboard. In this case, I have to describe the problems in your work without being able to write a comment or cross out a problem inside your text. Using Word uploads should make it easier for you to comprehend my comments and to improve your writing.

The **Writing Support Center** can be of help because there you can sit down with a proofreader and read your work together. Make notes on the mistakes you make in this evaluation, and later find a general **grammar textbook** of your choosing and research your weak areas to improve in them. Learning how to spot and solve a common grammatical problem is like being taught how to fish rather than being given a free fish to consume.

Part 2

Argumentative Essays

The second part of this book focuses on writing about politics and economics, or about class, ideology and power. The explanations of reading and writing methods shift to internet and library approaches, unlike the focus on a single text in Part 1. Sections on research philosophy, avoiding being overwhelmed by the quantity of information available online, and different types of readings available inside a library are suitable for any student learning about research writing. The part ends with a set of definitions and explanations of the key concepts in economics and politics that should assist students with writing about these fields.

Class, Ideology and Power Assignment

Write a 2-Page Essay that examines an economic or a political aspect of a cultural artifact of your choosing. You should choose an artifact that has a strong political or economic message, so that you can easily interpret what the message is and criticize it. Participation in the Editing Workshop counts as 10% of all short essays. The essay must include the following components:

1. A Thesis Statement that uses one of the key terms or concepts in the *Radical Agrarian Economics* reading. These terms are: monarchy, empire, feudalism, democracy, capitalism, totalitarianism, socialism, communism or agrarianism.
2. Paraphrase the narrative of the cultural artifact with a reader in mind that has never seen or read the artifact you are describing.
3. In addition to examining the primary artifact, properly use at least two secondary sources. One of these sources should be physical (book, journal, etc.), and the other should be electronic (digital archive materials, ebook, etc.).
4. Form a cohesive central argument and support your claims with logical points and evidence.
5. Proofread the essay for clarity, including fixing disruptive grammatical, spelling and punctuation problems.

The goal of this assignment is to offer a political or economic argument about a cultural artifact of your choosing. As citizens of the world, we all regularly perform research about politics when we prepare to vote, when we consider volunteering for local political positions, or when our lives are impacted by the political tide. We all also perform some micro-economic research before making a decision on purchasing a house or a car, finding a new job, or starting an independent business. The key terms utilized in this assignment are those used to categorize major economic and political systems in the world. Feudalism might be a thing of the past, but modern-day slavery or human trafficking is as relevant as it was at the peak of feudalism, and understanding the motivations of feudal owners explains many modern trends.

Nearly all of popular and highbrow cultural artifacts touch on economic or political themes related to these terms. Out of the top box office sales films of 2015, nearly all touch on at least one of these terms.

For example, *Star Wars: The Force Awakens* was about a rebellion against a tyrannical government. *Jurassic World* is in part an examination of capitalistic greed, as a resort is formed for the reach to display the dinosaurs leading to catastrophe. *Furious 7* touches on totalitarianism as the team are working to stop the improper use of the God's Eye, a surveillance tool that can track anybody through various digital devices (mass-surveillance was popular in the Soviet Union and other totalitarian regimes). A more comedic look at totalitarianism can be seen in the *Minions*, which shows a culture of creatures devoted to serving brutal dictators. *Mojin: The Lost Legend* glances at the monarchic political system, as the heroes search for the tomb of a Mongolian princess. If you look closely enough at most popular films, books and other artifacts with social messages, you will find some related themes or storylines to these very general terms. It should be easy to find a good topic as long as you avoid musical videos and other projects without such obvious political or economic content.

Internet and Library Research Methods

It might be easier for you to find sources that support your thesis if you choose an older cultural artifact that has been analyzed and criticized from a political or economic perspective by previous researchers. For example, if you study Tolstoy's *War and Peace*, you will find hundreds of scholarly books that have been written about this particular novel, biographies of Tolstoy, and various literary criticisms that interpret it from various theoretical perspectives. If you study an older political film, such as *Gone with the Wind*, it might be easier to find studies of the representation of slavery in it, and then to extrapolate from these to incorporate the feudalism concept. On the other hand, new films and books have been less criticized, so your argument is more likely to be innovative and unlike past arguments that might have been made on the same artifact. Before you choose the artifact to focus on, run a search to determine if you can find at least two of the required sources.

Searching for Sources at the Library

Technical Guide

Your initial search for sources should begin in the Library section of your college's website. There are several search options available. The quickest search is to type in a **keyword**. However, while you will see results quickly, it might take longer to sift through them than if you select the Advanced Search option and enter more specific parameters to limit your search. For example, let's say, you want to write a short research paper on *War and Peace*. If you type these words in the keyword field, unrelated books about various wars and peace agreements come up. If you type "Leo Tolstoy" in this general search, you will see the various books Tolstoy wrote. Only after scrolling through these irrelevant entries would you come across a source like: "*War and peace* [by] Leo Tolstoy. The Maude translation, backgrounds and sources, essays in criticism, edited by George Gibian." From this book, the "backgrounds and sources" and "essays in criticism" should all be excellent sources that would help you make a political argument connected to this novel. If you run the same general search for *Gone with the Wind*, the most relevant source might be, *Black Hollywood: From Butlers to Superheroes, the Changing Role of African American Men in the Movies* by Kimberly Fain. If you run an advanced search or add the term slavery as the keyword or subject to this title, you might find a more relevant book called, *Recasting "Gone with the Wind" in American Culture* by Darden Asbury Pyron. The catalog only gives a brief description of it, but you can find a longer description in the summary and reviews on Amazon, if you want to review this information before taking the book out from the library.

The assignment is to find one physical and one electronic source. For the electronic sources, you can run an **Advanced Search** and limit it by "Material Type" to "EBooks." This search will produce some better secondary sources because it is a specialized topic and only a few physical books on it are likely to be found in an average library system. In contrast, plenty of articles and chapters from scholarly books have been written on this subject, which are available for free through your Library account. A search turns up several very interesting sources including, *The Civil War as Global Conflict: Transnational Meanings of the American Civil War*, edited by David T. Gleeson and Simon Lewis, which has a chapter titled, "Race, Romance, and 'The spectacle of unknowing' in *Gone with the Wind*: A South African Response." You should be able to read an article like this in full through your library's digital database.

The above chapter in a book is available through Project Muse. If you know you are looking for an electronic resource, you can start the search from a different angle or through one of the **databases**. You can access the databases themselves by selecting Find > A-Z > and then the name of the database you are looking for. In addition to Project Muse, commonly used databases for humanities and social sciences are EB-

SCO Academic Search Complete and ProQuest. A wealth of scholarly information is available for free via these databases. A keyword search for EBooks will reach into many of these databases, rather than into only one of them.

To request a book that is available at a different campus library, a book request can be created through a library's website or from the front desk. It should take 3-4 business days to receive a book.

If you are having trouble finding books related to your subject in your college's library system, you should expand your search by looking for relevant books on WorldCat, which is an international library catalog that includes a significant portion of all published books, and is likely to return a lot more results on any narrow subject. For example, a search on WorldCat for "*Gone with the Wind* slavery" turns up, *Landscape of Slavery: The Plantation in American Art*. This book is available in a limited quantity of libraries, so it is unlikely it would be readily available at your library. If you are sure this book would have the strongest evidence to support your planned argument, you can request it through the Interlibrary Loan from other libraries outside of your library's immediate network. This is a free service, but it is likely to take longer for the book(s) to arrive at your campus, so you have to plan your research in advance. To make an interlibrary loan request, click on Library > Services > **Interlibrary Loan Request**.

Before taking any books out of a library, check on its **policies** regarding how long you can keep books for, what the penalties are for late-returns, if you can renew books, and the like.

Research Philosophy

If you were conducting research into a drug you were developing, the sources you would need would be studies that prove if similar drugs or approaches to cures have worked in the past. When you are researching a cultural artifact from a political or economic perspective, you are looking for evidence that helps you to prove a theory you have about the artifact. The proof is not going to be as technical, but rather based on historical and statistical facts or on patterns between a number of cultural artifacts. In a 2-Page Essay, you can only fit a few quotes, and some paraphrasing from the secondary sources you find. So, it is important that the sources you choose fit as closely as possible with the central argument. Spend more time on choosing the **relevant** sources, and it will be a lot easier to write the rest of this short research paper.

Most arguments have **multiple dimensions**. In the argument you are building for this essay, you are looking at a political or economic concept, at a cultural artifact, and you are making a link between them that proves your point of view. Thus, you might want to search for sources about the political concept not only as it pertains to the artifact, but also sources that examined this concept historically, theoretically or otherwise. In other words, if you're discussing communism, and you are unsure if you understand the term fully, it should help strengthen your argument if you search for sources about communism in practice or in theory. But, keep in mind that this is only a 2-Page Essay and you should not bring in irrelevant information that does not help to prove your Thesis.

Use the detached **Sherlock Holmes research style** when you are examining primary sources for evidence. Look at the cultural artifact as you would if it was a fossil and you were attempting to determine its age, significance, and the like. Avoid becoming emotionally involved in the narrative. It is irrelevant if it made you happy or sad unless you are discussing if the storyline had a tragic or a comic plotline. If you convince your reader(s) with evidence and a logical argument of your interpretation of the cultural artifact through the lens of the political or economic term, you are successfully solving a case, using the same philosophy as Sherlock would apply to deducing a murder mystery.

Internet Information Overload

To **paraphrase** the narrative in the artifact, you have to re-watch or re-read it. In addition, especially for films, you can consult plot summaries on Rotten Tomatoes or IMDb because in addition to various other benefits, they provide accurate spellings of character names that might not be intelligible even if you study a film very closely. If you use these sites, even if you do not take exact quotes from them, you should include entries for them in your Works Cited list. Scholarly encyclopedias are better equipped to handle classical books and films, and should be consulted if you choose an older project. Additionally, if you want to make **direct quotations** from a film, it might be helpful to obtain the **screenplay** version, which will provide the exact, transcribed quotes. If a printed book with the screenplay is not available, a digital screenplay might be more accessible.

The Internet is enormous, and there is more of it than meets the eye on the surface, as most of it is the iceberg in password protected, hidden servers. While some sources are **trustworthy**, you should avoid using sources that show an obvious bias or lack a close familiarity with the subject. For example, you should not use Rotten Tomatoes or IMDb as one of your central secondary sources, but rather only to check on the plotline, names and other pertinent information. Even some factual information on these relatively trustworthy sites might be inaccurate, and if you notice this, you should check the website administered by the makers of the movie for these details. Nearly all of the online or printed articles and books you will find through your college library's search function will be trustworthy because they will come from established journals, databases and publishers. So, it is safer to stick with these, rather than expending the search to the various freely available newspaper articles, blogs and various other sources of information that would come up if you googled the key terms.

Readings from the Library

Once you find the secondary physical sources relevant to your research project at the Library, you have to closely examine them to find the necessary evidence. If you are looking at a book, the **Index** can help you zoom in on the concept (communism, democracy etc.), artifact or another component that you are looking for. You also should start by reading the **headings** and sub-headings to spot the section that most closely fits the type of evidence that will prove your particular points. Especially when you are writing a very short research paper, you should choose short essays or segments from a book to closely read or mine for clues to avoid overloading yourself with information without finding something relevant. Scanning the materials for the relevant information is an important part of the research process. If you spend time **casually reading** several books vaguely related to your subject, this is a wasteful way to utilize your time as opposed to if you only spent an hour reading the **relevant sections** from a short but ideal article.

Bibliography

Walliman, Nicholas and Bousmaha Baiche. *Your Research Project: A Step-by-Step Guide for the First-Time Researcher.* London: Sage Publications, 2001.
Williams, Carol T. and Gary K. Wolfe. *Elements of Research: A Guide for Writers.* Chicago: Alfred Publishing Co., Inc., 1979.

Class, Ideology and Power Concepts

Many blockbuster films and popular books touch on political and economic concepts described below. There is an assumption that viewers
understand the allusions to the conflicts that these terms represent. In
other words, if a film is about a class conflict between the poor and
the rich, viewers who are familiar with Marxist or socialist theory see a
dimension of the film that might not be clear to other viewers. So, to
become better critical observers of cultural artifacts, we have to study
these terms and learn to utilize them in our research. The application
of political and economic dimensions to an analysis or an argument
about a cultural artifact is an established form of cultural and literary
criticism that is used in many dissertations and scholarly books. Thus,
there are plenty of secondary sources about well-known, older artifacts
that touch on these popular terms.

Class: Most modern statistics divide people into lower, middle and
upper classes. The definitions for each of these classes are given based
on the annual household or individual income levels. While logically,
these classes would make up thirds of the population, based on the cut
off points, in 2015, there were 20% of Americans in the lower class,
9% in the upper class, and the rest, 71%, were in the middle class, but
on the lower end of this middle class spectrum some families live on
$31,000 annually ("American Middle Class"). These numbers do not
account for the unemployed, and various other factors that might be
a truer representation of American society. In Marxist economics, the
classes are divided in two, the proletariat (working people) and the
bourgeoisie (idle and wealthy people that make money from interests,
speculation, and other sources that are not directly involved with the
production process). From the Marxist perspective, most Americans
are in the proletariat because only a small percentage of the upper class
does not need to be actively involved in producing goods or services.

Ideology: A system of beliefs that makes a political or an economic
theory or national policy. Communism, democracy, monarchy and
many of the other terms on this list are ideologies. While people inside
a system with a dominant ideology might believe that it is the only
rational way of governing or conducting business relations, it is merely
a set of ideas that might not be as good as another valid system of beliefs. Most wars have an ideological basis and result when contradictory

ideologies clash across foreign borders.

Power: The person, political body or another entity that has control over a government or an economic system has power. Power is typically defended with military, police and other types of forces. Power can change hands between political leaders, political parties, and between different world superpowers. It is present in various forms and has various significances in different contexts.

Politics: The political field of study examines forms of governance and how a governing system functions. The three branches of government in a democracy and the one branch of power in a monarchy are all studied in this far-reaching field. Studying election fraud, new proposed legislation, and various other political ideas all can be found here.

Economics: The study of production and consumption of goods and services. This field includes examinations of the differences between socialism and capitalism, as well as touching on some of the other key terms here. When we discuss cultural artifacts as commodities that are created with a buying market in mind, we are engaging in economic theory.

Monarchy: A system of government where a King or a Queen has the dominant power that is usually distributed between three branches of government in a democratic system: judicial (the courts), legislative (the Senate/ Congress), and executive (the President and his or her cabinet). In other words, the King or representatives chosen by the King (or Queen) rule over the courts, create the laws, and decide on all of the executive military, economic and other key decisions. In a constitutional monarchy, (i.e. United Kingdom0, the monarch acts as the head of state, while congressional bodies and the courts act as mostly separate branches that can check or balance the monarch's decisions.

Empire: When a country is victorious over other countries in military battles or forms alliances with other countries, it can become an Empire with control over other territories outside of its own borders. The conquest over other territories is called colonialism, and the practice of overpowering foreign nations is called colonialization. It is currently considered unethical to engage in warfare for the purpose of colonizing other countries, but Britain, the United States and other empires still hold onto the countries they colonized, making them into territories, or fully integrating them into their own political structure, as happened with Hawaii.

Feudalism: "In the feudal system, the king guarantees certain protections and rights to the serfs, while in the slave system the slaves do not have any rights in exchange for giving their lives and labor… The peasants needed this safety net after the fall of the Roman Empire because the Saracen and Viking invaders were brutal, and there were many other minor battles and quarrels that made avoiding starvation difficult. Since most of the peasants were not literate, and only wanted to have the minimum required to survive, they were willing to live in extreme poverty in exchange for defense during warfare and the promise of heaven in the afterlife. Eventually, private land and property ownership led to the evolution of capitalism, or the private control over land and resources by corporations, instead of the Crown" (Faktorovich 97-8).

Democracy: "In democracy, individual rulers can be taken out of office, but the bourgeoisie still maintain control over the government and act in the interests of the rich and not of the poor. Change of presidents can lull a public into a false sense of revolution or rotation of power, so that the underlying problems appear to not be as overwhelming as the problems in feudalism or monarchic systems" (Faktorovich 129).

Capitalism: An economic system in which trade is controlled by private owners that lead the economy with the decisions they take. Capitalism came after feudalism when merchants started profiting from selling goods they were producing or purchasing from serfs. Later they started buying up the monarch's lands and started private businesses outside of the feudal system. Staunch capitalists argue that this system works best when it has minimum government oversight, but most capitalist systems are governed by some policies against monopolies and unfair competition.

Totalitarianism: Complete control over the government and economy by a single individual or group of individuals. This system can only have a single party or a single ideology that it supports, while it negates or suppresses all contrary opinions or actions.

Socialism: An ideology that supports ownership of the means of production by the producers, community, or the proletariat, as opposed to by a bank or a business owner who is not involved in the production process.

Communism: An ideology that supports public ownership of the means of production, and the distribution of wealth according to needs rather than based on capitalist competition between the members in a society.

Agrarianism: An ideology that supports subsistence living of privately owned land, including working the land with a family unit and selling the resulting products locally. According to Allan Carlson's *The New Agrarian Mind: The Movement Towards Decentralist Thought in Twentieth-Century America*, the New Agrarian model means:

- the elimination of national and international markets in food and fiber, so that local producers would grow for local use;
- the elimination of local markets, as well, since no market mechanism could value items such as topsoil, ecosystem, farm family, or community;
- the use of differential taxation to insure the wide distribution of property;
- government-subsidized loans for the purchase of farms by property-less families;
- national control on production;
- governmental controls on commodity prices to ensure a fair balance between farming income and necessary expenses;
- state-imposed limits on the application of technology to farming;
- tariffs on food and fiber commodities high enough to discourage import of products that could be grown locally;
- the declaration of a "right" to be a small farmer, within "limits" that were obvious and reasonable;
- the creation of a new kind of money that "does not lie about value," but rather created "a decent balance between what people earn and what they pay";
- and [perhaps most realistically], a change in the way professors of agriculture were paid, where half of their compensation would come from produce off a grant of land for their own productive use (Carlson 193-94).

Give these concepts some thought before you choose the artifact to focus on. Read more about the term that you are most interested in, so that you can discuss it fluidly in your essay.

Bibliography

Faktorovich, Anna. *Radical Agrarian Economics: Wendell Berry and Beyond*. Atlanta: Anaphora Literary Press, 2015.

"The American Middle Class Is Losing Ground: No Longer the Majority and Falling Behind Financially." Washington DC: *Pew Research Center*. 9 December 2015. Web. 17 September 2016.

Carlson, Allan. *The New Agrarian Mind: The Movement Towards Decentralist Thought in Twentieth-Century America*. New Brunswick: Transaction Publishers, 2000.

Part 3

Supporting Claims
and Anticipating Objections

The third part analyzes the structure of a logical argument. It begins with an explanation of what the logical point of view is in contrast with an emotional or an illogical one. Then, the common logical fallacies are summarized, with an explanation as to why they should be avoided. Then, a section explains why it is important to support all claims presented in a research paper with solid evidence from primary or secondary sources. The frequently used introduction structures are digested, so that writers who might otherwise be froze with procrastination can start their essays with one of these effective introductory structures. The last section explains the need to anticipate the likely objections readers will have as they read an essay. It also guides students as to how best to deal with conflicting views among the sources reviewed or among potential readers. Based on information gathered while grading a lot of research papers, these topics are especially necessary early on in this type of a class. Without this information, students are prone to present illogical, or ill-supported arguments.

Research writing is always performed to convince the reader in the argument it is conveying. This applies to research performed in scientific experiments and into literary texts. Even if you simply want to narrate your research project, you are defending your methods and outcomes. And if your research project contradicts prior findings, you have to actively argue against earlier conclusions. The evidence you find in primary and secondary sources should all be relevant to proving your Thesis or central argument. However, simply finding relevant evidence is not enough for effective research writing. You have to do your best to convince readers with logical and masterful presentation and analysis of the evidence. Too many writers digress into unrelated materials, personal reflections, or simply commit logical fallacies that undermine their research. Even if you find less evidence to support your argument, if you follow the guidelines of proper research writing, you will be more likely to convince readers. This is because readers who are distracted by a lack of clarity or sense that the writer's logic is flawed are unlikely to fall for even the best of intentions. Have you ever listened to an argument where one of the parties is clearly omitting key information or running in circles around the same point? That person might not be aware that he or she is committing these errors, and the only way to improve his or her ability to make stronger researched arguments is to study this section.

Logical Point of View

An "argument is a special kind of discourse, in which a claim is made that one or more particular statements should be accepted as true, or probably true, on the grounds that certain other statements are true. Put another way: by the process of reasoning, using the operation of logic, a conclusion is inferred from the statements given" (Walliman 122). A claim is an assertion of truth. The definition above allows for the possibility that the claim might be untrue because even things that are believed to be true today, might be proven to be untrue in the future. The rest of the definition states that arguments typically use what is proven to be true to prove a new assertion that the writer hypothesizes is true. In other words, the argument itself is not performing research to prove if something is true, but instead draws conclusions about truthfulness by logically connecting a new concept to one that has been proven to be true.

Logical arguments have been used to convince people in various, potentially unprofitable for individuals, government or economic systems, such as capitalism or monarchy. These ideologies are composed of a series of claims that are all proven to be true by association. If you successfully question and argue against the truthfulness of the central claims in each of these ideologies, such as the value of money or divine rights of a monarch, the rest of the arguments tied to these assertions also fall apart and you end up defeating the whole ideology in your argument. Even if your intention is not the creation of a New World Order, logical arguments can help anybody from a car salesperson to a neuro researcher.

The structure of a logical argument is a formula that you might be familiar with from previous English classes. An argument must include:

- "the **introduction** of the research problem"
- "the **examination and analysis** of the problem"
- "the presentation of the **findings**" (frequently preceded by indicators such as: because, as shown by, for the reason that)

- "the analysis and **conclusions**" (frequently preceded by indicators such as: therefore, thus, consequently) (Walliman 123).

If you are missing one of these elements, your argument will not be fully formed, and will not be as convincing. For example, if you fail to introduce the problem you are tackling, and simply jump into your research findings, your reader will be lost and will not understand how the evidence you are presenting is related to your Thesis. And no argument can stand without evidence and analysis at its center. The best conclusion without the logical proof to support that it is truthful cannot be considered an argument. At the same time, if you leave your evidence as you found them without drawing conclusions from them, the evidence alone cannot complete an argument as it might lead the reader to a different conclusion than the one you intended.

Logical Fallacies

Logical fallacies are reasoning errors. In other words, they are not errors in analysis or research method, but rather are errors in the way an argument is made. A logical fallacy typically signifies that the argument attempted has become illogical because of this flaw. The rules of these fallacies assume a logical and well-informed reader that is likely to be appalled by illogic or unfair debate methods.

Omission: If you omit a crucial detail to prove the veracity of your claim, it is likely to lead to an untrue conclusion. For example, if you are researching the effect of rat poison on rats, and you omit to consider prior findings about the deadly effects of rat poison, your conclusion will have a major untruth at its root. It is unlikely that anybody would believe you that rat poison is healthy for rats, but if you substitute it with a less obvious idea, you might be able to fool some readers. You have to assume that your readers are well-informed in the field you are writing about and that they will detect any serious omissions and that this will dismantle the rest of your argument. No researcher can include all of the previous research in a complex subject, but there are some obvious and relevant truths or facts that must be stated.

Presumption: Asserting what is true or untrue is at the heart of all arguments. Thus, if you presume that something is true without verifying via prior research that it has been proven to be true, you are starting your argument on a false claim, and thus dooming its conclusion to be untruthful as a result. For example, if you start your argument with the presumption that George Orwell was a communist without checking if there is proof to support this argument, it will be easy to contradict the rest of your analysis and your conclusions simply by pointing out evidence to the contrary or that Orwell was actually anti-communist. Whenever you build a claim on things you presume to be true stop to ask yourself if you have researched these truths enough to be certain of their truthfulness.

Generalization: This problem occurs frequently in beginners' research papers. It is easy to make grand statements about the world or people in general. You might have read similar statements in philosophical texts or in literature. For example, Leo Tolstoy started *Anna Karenina*, a novel about infidelity, with: "Happy families are all alike; every unhappy family is unhappy in its own way." The bulk of this book deals with the details or with specific evidence of what could have happened to a woman that was unfaithful and decided to obtain a divorce from her spouse. Thus, thus generalization is more like an introductory claim of wider truth, rather than merely an unsupported generalization. *Anna Karenina* is a very long book and fiction by definition does not have to be truthful. The problem of generalization is more obvious when students generalize in short 2-6 page research papers. Can anybody prove in a non-fiction, logical argument that all happy families are alike? Some happy families do not have any children, while others have dozens. Some happy families are open marriages, while others are hyper-committed. Only if we define "happiness" in a family with strict parameters, can we then conclude that his narrow definition of happiness can only include the families we have pre-defined as qualified for happiness. In other words, if we presume that a family can be proven to be happy if it contains two children, committed parents, a suburban house, two cars, and a high average smile rate, then sure, all of the happy families in this category will be alike. But this type of re-defining of a term to fit with your argument is illogical and unhelpful if we are trying to arrive at a sincere truth. Your argument can be strengthened if you choose a narrower topic that can be defended in the amount of pages you are allowed. The happiness of all families is too general because the components are too encompassing as nearly everybody on the planet is a member of a family and has experienced some degree of happiness. On the other hand, researching contentment of characters in a novel and what causes it is a project that is narrow enough. If you want to talk about humanity at-large or about groups of people, these claims have to be supported with statistical evidence that prove that your assertion is not merely a generalization, but rather a fact.

Circular Argument: Beginner researchers also frequently make the mistake of repeatedly restating their assertions or conclusions, instead of leading the argument through the evidence and analysis needed to prove their veracity. Frequently, the central Thesis is a generalization in these tailspins. The researcher proclaims something like that all happy families are happy in the same way, and then keeps repeating this generalization instead of building the case for it. Generalization and circular argumentation typically go together because a general claim cannot be logically defended. It can only appear to be supported by allowing the argument to repeat itself numerous times until it is repeated yet again in the conclusion. While the researcher attempting this illogical or fallacious argument might be convinced that he or she succeeded in proving a Thesis, most readers are flabbergasted after reading these nonsensical repetitions. A close reader is certain that he or she has just been deceived by an unskilled trickster. So, avoid repeating assertions without building proof on top of them to carry your readers to your logical conclusions.

Either/or: If something is true, something else does not have to be untrue. To prove an argument that a claim is true, you cannot merely prove that something else is untrue. Here is an example of this fallacy: "We can either stop eating chicken, or all chickens will die." It would take an extreme ecological crisis for all chickens all over the world to go extinct. Human consumption of chicken alone currently seems unlikely to lead to their extinction because so many of them are bred in poultry enterprises. In general, focus on proving that your claim is correct, rather than on what other claims might be incorrect unless you are arguing against them without breaking logical laws. You might be able to prove that humans should stop eating chicken by describing how chicken are mistreated during their production. You might even be able to prove (if needed evidence existed) that all chickens will die. But mixing the two in a grand, unsupportable statement that positions them as opposites, wherein only one can be true, when this is not the case is a fallacy.

Emotional Appeal: Logical arguments should not rely on emotional appeals, either positive or negative. In fiction, writers always sway readers by describing heart-wrenching emotional situations that appeal to the readers' sympathy. The fiction writer can convince readers to cheer for the hero to win by showing that he is not only in deadly peril but also heartbroken about losing the love of his life. In non-fiction research writing such appeals to the loss of love by the writer or a character being described is frequently irrelevant or illogical. For example, if you are arguing that a rap music video depicts gender bias when it shows women being mistreated, it would be an erroneous emotional appeal for you to point out that all female readers should be afraid that they will be mistreated in a similar way. Readers might respond by feeling fear, and thus their emotions are engaged. However, educated readers will detach themselves from the fear and will conclude that the writer is attempting to manipulate their emotions instead of presenting evidence to support the claim. Some advertisers might stoop to low, negative emotional appeals by bringing in starving and crying children, unrelated to the product being sold. Positive emotions, such as pride, can also be triggered in political campaigns. A product or a political candidate might be, in essence, counter-productive or counter-intuitive to the viewer, but the emotional appeal can confuse the intellect and allow emotions guide a decision. While emotional appeals might work in politics and advertising, when you are writing a research paper in a class, you are typically graded on your ability to make a logical and detached argument, rather than on your ability to sway emotional responses.

Supporting Claims

What Makes for Strong Supporting Evidence? The size, scope, subject and other components of your research project determine the type of evidence that is likely to convince readers of your position. Some research requires statistical evidence, while other types of research rely on quotations from other texts. You should read research similar to your own to figure out the types of evidence that is typically considered as adequate in a given field. In general, relevant scholarly articles and books about the narrow subject are trustworthy sources. The primary and secondary sources you find should be truthful or trustworthy so that you can use them to build your claim that your own argument is also truthful. These sources have to be relevant because bringing in unrelated evidence does nothing to support your primary objective in the essay. In other words, you are making an environmental argument and you bring in a book about gender bias, the digression into an unrelated subject will only degrade your argument. In other words, think about an essay as an assignment to build a pyramid out of yellow blocks. If you add red blocks to the pyramid, you are not meeting the requirements of the assignment, just as if you left the pyramid unfinished.

Theory or Research First? Should you begin with an idea or by reading relevant sources about the subject and then developing a theory based on these findings? This depends on your personal preferences. For me, it's easier to review the relevant secondary sources first until I have a sufficient number of quotes, paraphrases and other types of evidence on a subject. Then, I review these findings, and I draw a theory or my Thesis based on what the analysis of this evidence indicates. Other researchers begin with a **hypothesis** or a statement regarding what they are setting out to prove to be true. They then actively look for evidence that proves this hypothesis to be correct, instead of looking for all relevant evidence and allowing it to speak for itself. Starting with a theory is necessary in pharmaceutical research, for example, where a researcher has to be looking for a certain type of new drug to find evidence to support its suitability. Political writers that write propaganda for political campaigns also start with a narrow theory and have to gather evidence to prove it. If you feel passionately about an idea, you can set up your research project with the goal of proving its veracity. If you feel passionately about learning what the truth is, regardless of its ethical, moral or legal implications, it is best to conduct the research first.

Classification: When researchers are deciding on what evidence is relevant to their analysis, they typically classify a series of related subjects into classes. For example, under the larger class of literature, there is popular and highbrow literature, there is also science fiction and fantasy, and there are short stories and novels. Each of these two sets of categories is a set if branches in the tree of literary classification. If you are studying fantasy novels, you are looking at categories of pop fiction, the long novel form, and under speculative fiction. If you think through all of these sub-branches, you can search for secondary sources related to each of them and not only to the narrow subject that is at the tip of your inquiry. There might be some great scholarly books about communism in all novels, and only a few about communism in fantasy novels. Classifying subjects will also help you to exclude unrelated branches from your research, so that you do not consider communism in poetry or non-fiction as well, if these might lead you to very different results.

Analogy: An argument can be strengthened by drawing analogies between your argument or claim and a parallel argument that has already been proven to be true. This is unlike arguing that if something is true, something else must be untrue. In an analogy, you are comparing similar theories with the help of evidence that show their similarity. In addition, an analogy can help readers who might not understand a new theory you are introducing grasp it by relating it to a familiar theory they have been convinced by previously. **Similes** are analogies that compare things with the help of the words like or as. An abstract comparison between objects without the use of as or like is called a **metaphor**. More generally, comparing any two professions to each other or showing the similarity between any two political theories are all examples of analogies.

Cause and Effect: Another common component of argumentative writing is an explanation of how a cause is related to an effect. Humans understand the world as related via complex cause and effect systems. In the ecosystem, a shark might eat a smaller fish, which in turn eats floating plant matter, etc. The earth heating up might lead to the effect of a volcano erupting. If it's raining somewhere; then, somewhere else water evaporated. Thus, it is only natural to attempt to explain the causes of a phenomenon in nature, a strange outcome in literature, or a catastrophic war in history. To do so, the researcher has to narrate what the cause and the effect are and how they are related.

Introduction Types

Many writers experience writer's block because they do not know how to begin writing. Using one of the common introduction types will help you to start the essay by following standard, formulaic components. This is one of the reasons for most of the formulaic elements of research writing. Knowing what elements are required for a suitable conclusion, speeds up the process of writing it and allows it to be as convincing as it can be. Especially when you begin with the research instead of starting with a hypothesis, you will want to write the introduction after you have composed the body of the essay where you analyze the relevant evidence.

New Perspective: One of these formulaic introductions is used to explain that the argument is a new view on an old problem. There are only so many possible arguments about the human condition, about literature, about culture, or about all the other concepts or elements of existence or the world around us. Unless you are conducting research into a narrow subject that is entirely innovative, you are probably presenting a new perspective on an established argumentative line of reasoning. For example, when the Wright Brothers took flight, there were many other innovative pilots and engineers before them that had developed other versions of airplanes and flight theory. Even when a research project appears to be extremely groundbreaking, it typically stems from many related perspectives, theories and conclusions. So, in an introduction that stresses the relationship of your idea to other ideas before it, you should start by summarizing this history of ideas, and then explain how your perspective is similar and how it differs from the others.

Enhancement or Refutation of an Error: Another common reason to start an argument is if you believe that the previous conclusions on an assertion were inaccurate or untrue. For example, if you read a scholarly article related to your subject, and you notice logical fallacies, gaps in the research or erroneous deductions, you can focus your own argument on disproving this earlier analysis. You can also enhance an earlier argument by adding dimensions to it, or expanding the scope of the study, or focusing in on one of the less proven components of the subject. In this introduction type, you have to start by summarizing the central argument that you are refuting or enhancing. Then, explain why the argument is erroneous or needs enhancement. And then, summarize the key points you will use in your research paper to enhance or correct this earlier argument.

Narrative: If your research project is attempting to prove an argument that has been established as truthful in the past, you should opt for the narrative introduction. In this structure, instead of explaining what you are arguing against, you simply narrate the plotline, the history, or the story of how an experiment was carried out. In formal research, a narrative such as this is called the **statement of fact**. In other words, it states the key known truths related to the Thesis.

Anticipating Objections and Conflicting Points of View

Before you write a research paper, spend some time thinking about why some of your readers might disagree with your argument. This process can be assisted by reading essays or books that demonstrate or prove a theory that is contradictory to your own. Both arguments might have some validity. If you mention the conflicting theory in your essay and explain why you believe your argument holds more truth, then your reader will notice that you have fairly weighed the options before reaching your own conclusion. In addition, weighing contradictory arguments will help you to avoid including generalizations that can be proven to be untrue when other points of view are taken into account. Including too much information and supporting evidence for an opposing perspective can do you a disservice of convincing readers that you are wrong, but including just enough evidence to explain the other logical alternatives will help to strengthen your position. An argument that assumes all other perspectives are erroneous without proving why this is the case is pompous and unlikely to sway anybody from the other camp. Any politician will tell you that if you flatter your opponent by pointing out that you agree with some of the components of their argument before explaining to them how it is wrong on a larger scale, you are much more likely to win the debate. The main goal of a research paper is to convince readers that your argument is truthful. In addition to knowing why you are correct, you have to explain why the other side is incorrect, as there are two sides to most coins.

Works Cited

Tolstoy, Leo. *Anna Karenina*. Constance Garnett, Tr. Project Gutenberg. 22 February 2013. Web. 25 September 2016.

Walliman, Nicholas and Bousmaha Baiche. *Your Research Project: A Step-by-Step Guide for the First-Time Researcher*. London: Sage Publications, 2001.

Part 4

Clarity in Writing Style

Once writers have a general direction for their research, it is time for them to learn the methods that help them write clearly. Even the best arguments and evidence can be lost if a writer coats it with confusion, nonsense, or grammatical errors. The common clarity-related topics covered here are: clichés, empty abstractions, failure to comprehend terms a writer utilizes, lack of contextualization, vagueness, and lack of transitions. Clichés or other empty language detracts from an argument by referring to unrelated concepts instead of focusing on the subject at hand. Another frequent problem is a student's failure to fully understand the terms he or she uses in an essay, and their resultant misuse. Jarring jumps between unrelated topics also makes some essays unreadable.

Clarity of expression is a crucial component of writing because if the research paper is not legible or comprehendible, a reader cannot understand the argument that it is trying to relay. Revision is necessary to make even the best essay easier to read. Some grammar books suggest eliminating passive voice and long sentences to improve clarity. But the shortening of sentences and an access of active voice has led to a sea of watered-down popular novels that have hyper-short sentences, paragraphs, and words. And the lack of passive voice can make a story into a purely action-based narration, deleting passive reflection and abstract contemplation. And passivity is not necessarily more confusing for the reader. Here is an example:

Active Voice: The girl [subject] is carrying [verb] an umbrella [object].
Passive Voice: An umbrella [object] is being carried [verb] by the girl [subject].

In these two short sentences, the second, passive option seems to be unnecessarily verbose. But, in nineteenth century novels, passive sentences frequently carried symbolic, metaphorical or other significances that the word order helped to relay.

Active Voice: The mysterious girl, who is running from the scene, is carrying the black umbrella with holes in its sides.

Passive Voice: The black umbrella with holes in its sides is being carried by the mysterious girl who is running from the scene.

Reversing the order of the sentence into the active voice puts a stress on the girl. But if the line is from a mystery novel and the umbrella was just used as a weapon in a murder; then, the umbrella needs to hold the central, stressed position at the beginning of the sentence. As you can see some common rules about what makes for clear writing do not apply to every possible type of essays or other writing genres.

Because there are few generic rules that assure a clear writing style, the best way to check for clarity or to notice potential mistakes is to slowly read and **re-read** your work. Most people struggle with reading their own work with a critical eye. One strategy to avoid this problem is by **reading it aloud** to hear the errors in the text that might escape you if you skim it, assuming that you heard it play out correctly in your mind as you were writing it. If you read the error, you should automatically feel as if something is wrong with the sentence. We are an auditory society and many of us watch more TV than read books. Even if you try to read a misspelled word, it should sound unlike how you have previously heard it sound on the airways or TV networks.

If you are unsure about the spelling of a word as you are writing it, you should check the dictionary just to make sure the meaning matches the spelling. If you check it a couple of times, it will help you remember the correct spelling.

The time you spent on reading your work should also help you come up with new analysis or new relevant ideas to strengthen your argument. Especially in research writing, when you pull evidence from a few different sources together, you might see some parallels and conclusions that they are pointing to, but all of it will mix and process as a whole better after you read the draft. While two quotes might have appeared unrelated when you first wrote it, on a second reading, you might suddenly realize how they are connected and why this connection strengthens your main point.

Clichés

Clichés are problematic because they introduce an abstract concept that seems to be making a logical point, but because they are always generalizations, they are logical fallacies, or untrue. Here are two examples:

Actions speak louder than words.
You can't judge a book by its cover.

Think about the first one logically. First, it is saying that actions can "speak," and that they can do it better than words. Unless the action in question is speech, walking, jumping, running or performing other active verbs is unlikely to be a better form of speech. Jumping might be louder than speaking, if you jump on an acoustic stage or the like. And some words might simply be more impactful or powerful than some actions, depending on what the words and actions are. If you insert this statement into a casual conversation, your listeners will understand your intended meaning. But if you insert this cliché into a research paper, it is likely that your readers will attempt to interpret the deeper meaning because the research context does not typically include casual reflections.

In the second example, a reader hunting for a deeper meaning might ask you, as the researcher, about the fact that books with beautiful covers typically selling better than books with simple or unflattering covers. And, going further, you might be asked if beautiful people statistically might succeed better in life and relationships. Further still, you might be asked why you are commanding your reader to stop judging book covers, or why you are telling the reader that he or she is unable to evaluate a book cover. In other words, if you use generalizations and refer to all books or all speakers, there are too many potential flaws or weaknesses in your argument. And, if you are not making an argument about books or speakers, you probably should not bring in unrelated allusions or metaphors into the research paper.

Empty Abstractions

Clichés are also problematic because they are a type of empty abstractions. Abstract art has been popular across this past century. Picasso drew abstract shapes to represent people. Jackson Pollock tossed buckets of paint onto white sheets on the floor. A research paper should not include these types of abstractions, just like they are out of place in a test in a classical painting class. Even a concept as apparently simple as "honesty" can be too abstract for a research paper. All arguments are attempting to prove that their claims are true. But, honesty in general is difficult to define because most arguments contradict other arguments. In other words, if the argument a Republican is making is true, it does not mean that an opposing argument a Democrat is making is false. If there are two sides to a debate, it would be strange if one of the sides was telling a pure untruth while the other was relaying an exact truth. And if a husband misleads his wife by omitting to tell her about an affair, this does not necessarily mean that he was dishonest with her. In other words, if you want to talk about honesty or dishonesty, you should relate the evidence and explain why they are truthful or untruthful instead of simply claiming that one of the sides is dishonest without this supporting evidence.

Ideally, you will be able to avoid abstractions all together in research writing unless you are researching an abstract concept. And even if the concept under examination is abstract, you should still strive to find **concrete examples** to defend it. Describing real or observable actions and objects proves a claim more efficiently than defending it in abstract terms. In other words, proving that a cow walked across a lawn with a video of the cow in action is easier than attempting to argue that in some hypothetical scenario something catastrophic can happen outside anybody's house. When you are writing about fiction or non-fiction, quotes taken out of a work are concrete examples, while your reflections about abstract messages without this sound proof are empty abstractions.

At the same time, some abstract thinking is necessary to explain an economic, political, cultural or literary **theory**. Interpreting the meaning of brief quotes out of a novel takes some abstract or un-concrete extrapolation. If you read the segments where you depart into abstractions, you should be able to spot when the abstracted ideas might be strengthened if they were replaced with solid examples.

Comprehension of Terms

Most research papers utilize some complex terminology or vernacular common in a given research field. These terms typically compress a sentence of meaning into themselves. Thus, you should not shy away from using difficult terms. But you have to check the dictionary or a textbook on their exact meaning before employing them. If you mix up "consumer" with "producer," an educated reader will either spot the mistake or will be confused by the illogical statement around this word. If you do not want to check the dictionary, you should not attempt using words you do not completely understand because it is better to avoid a mistake and to add a longer description instead of the short term. Even if you are writing a two-page paper, familiarizing yourself with commonly used terms in a field such as economics, politics, or literary analysis is a worth-while effort.

Contextualization

Even if you comprehend all of the terms you are using, if you do not put them into the fitting context, they will not convey the intended meaning. At times brevity makes for clearer communication. But, at other times, being too brief and too direct can mislead or confuse a reader. For example, if you bring up an example of a general from an obscure war, you have to explain the sides that fought in the conflict and other pertinent facts before the reader will be able to relate these details to the central argument. It is particularly important to explain the context when you bring in new information that is not tied to other content you are covering. Obviously, if you allow the context explanation to go too far afield, you are digressing from your central argument. So, you have to find a balance between explaining new concepts and focusing on your central claims. Context is also needed to explain the relationship between an artifact and an abstract political or economic concept, or with other artifacts. For example, if you are discussing the term "bourgeoisie," you have to contextualize it by classifying it as one of the two opposing sides in communist economic theory, one that stands against the proletariat. Discussing the bourgeoisie or the leisurely rich exploiters without comparing them to the working proletariat would leave your reader puzzled about this term, possibly questioning why you are not simply calling them rich people or the upper class. Think about what contextual information you needed to understand a given term, concept or example, and then insert this explanation into your essay.

Vagueness

Logical arguments should not be vague. Generalization is an obvious form of vagueness. Logical arguments should not generalize about a group of books, literature in general, or other categories without proof. But beyond generalization, any statements that fail to strike at a narrow point at the heart of your Thesis should be discarded. You should also strive to express certainty in your conclusions rather than presenting them as a "maybe" or a potential truth. Uncertainty about truthfulness might be a politically correct approach, but it weakens a researched argument. Broad claims that cannot be supported in the few pages devoted to a research paper are another form of vagueness. Clichés can be an example of broad claims that attempt to prove things such as that it is better to avoid judging a book by its cover. But any claim that is too ambitious for the allowed pages can come across as vague or unclear because it is unsupportable. Instead of relying on vague, abstract or unclear and unsupported speculations, all narrow and precise claims should be supported with concrete and specific evidence and the logical analysis of this evidence. And if you are comparing or drawing a parallel between a film or a book and the arguments from a political or economic theory, you have to give quotes, names, or specific narrative summaries of the main points that relate to both, rather than simply saying they are similar.

Transitions

Even if you present evidence and fully analyze it, a lack of proper transitions can make an essay unclear, confusing and overall weak. Including different ideas without explaining the relationship between them is like wearing jeans, a fancy top and a royal-silk hat in un-matching, clashing colors. But, while an odd outfit can be explained as experimental, abstract, or simply unique, the same excuses cannot be made for a research paper. It is natural and necessary to find evidence that falls into three different categories for a short 5-paragraph research paper with three body paragraphs. Each of the paragraphs should have a different point it is working to prove. If all three body paragraphs were proving the same central point without variation, there would be no reason to separate these into paragraphs. You decided to separate them into paragraphs because you saw how the ideas differed, so now you have to explain these differences at the start of new paragraphs so that the reader understands the organizational structure. Within each of the paragraphs, you are likely to have unique bits of evidence (quotes or paraphrasing) and their analysis. The analysis should include an explanation regarding how the different bits fit together or how they prove different parts of your larger argument. You might not need entire sentences dedicated to making these connections, but rather simply words such as: therefore, whereas, hence, and thus. The idea is for the transitions to become a natural and essential though also mostly invisible part of the essay, rather than to have them become a major portion of it. The use of "whereas" and other single-word transitions also help with clarity at the sentence-level, so that ideas in a sentence are logically connected. Transitions also help at the end of the introduction, the start of the body and the start of the conclusion to signal that you are moving between these parts. For example, if you start the conclusion with "in summary," your reader will understand that what follows is an important summative statement and will be prepared to pay attention to your explanation. Traditionally, the topic or first sentences in each of the body paragraphs serve as transitions as they introduce the new idea that will be introduced in a given paragraph and how it differs from those explained in other paragraphs. When you read your essay aloud, it should become obvious which parts need better transitions as the ideas will seem poorly linked to other ideas around them or you might be left with a general sense of confusion. If you are confused regarding the relationship of ideas in your own essay, what chance do your readers have?

Part 5

The Rhetorical Form of a Research Essay

Here writers will learn about the formula that makes up any research essay as a genre. Once they understand that there is a mathematical logic to how a research essay is structured, the essay becomes more approachable and easier to attempt. The modes of discourse further categorize different types of writing and explain what is involved in the different types of essays professors might assign not only in this, but also in future college classes. The section on organization begins with an explanation that a research paper can also be broken down into these components: background, purpose, evidence, analysis, and conclusions. Then, these and other components, such as the connection between claims, supporting evidence and warrants, are explained. The "Gender Bias Essay Assignment" is introduced here, together with guidelines for its completion.

Whenever you are asked to write a project in college or at your job, it is always important to start by understanding the genre into which the project falls. A research paper is very different from other rhetorical structures such as a newspaper article or a narrative essay. The most common way to determine the required structure in a genre is buy closely studying the components of a few examples. Finding a book about how to write in a given genre should help if you are planning to do a lot of writing and need additional guidance. There are numerous books written about how to write novels, newspaper content, or most of the other genres that make up significant markets for writers. This section is a brief summary of these repeating elements of a research paper.

Genre

Target Audience: One of the components that puts a project into the research paper genre is the intended target audience. Research papers can be written for scholars, teachers, professors, or for fellow students, but they are not usually written for a popular audience or for casual readers. Research is intended to dive deep into a problem and to draw new conclusions from a collection of evidence. Because target audiences differ, you should give some thought about the familiarity of your particular audience with the subject you are covering. Is it likely that they have read the books you are reviewing and analyzing or do you need to summarize their content in case somebody in the audience if unfamiliar with the findings that you are using as the basis for your own research? When deciding about the type of audience on the other side of the paper, you should consider their education level, exposure to the types of content you are discussing, age, regional knowledge and any other descriptive components that might change their reading of your research. If you know the types of people that make up your audience, you can also anticipate their likely objections. There are statistics available that prove if most suburban women have a different perspective on a given political topic in contrast with urban men, and the like. These types of demographics are essential for marketers and election coordinators, but considering them will also help make a college research paper more persuasive. You should be aware that your audience for a college paper is your professor and your fellow students, and you should allow this to guide you as to what might persuade this audience more efficiently.

Purpose: It is important to have a purpose in mind when you start writing in any genre. The purpose separates different types of writing into genres. For example, if your purpose is to describe, it is likely that you are writing a narrative essay that primarily summarizes information, events or other elements on a given subject. The purpose of a research paper is to argue for the truthfulness of your claims. Unlike other types of argumentative essays, a research paper heavily relies on evidence from primary and secondary sources or on the findings from a practical study or experiment. The goal is to convince readers that your interpretation of the evidence is correct and that your findings should be trusted.

Literature Review: Most research papers include at least a brief literature review. This is a review of the key secondary sources available on a given topic. In a dissertation, the literature review might take up an entire chapter or a significant portion of a chapter, as most of the relevant critical studies have to be summarized and evaluated for their relevance, timeliness, correctness and other perspectives. In the conclusion of a lengthy literature review, the author explains how his or her unique study is necessary because previous studies in this field neglected or have not sufficiently explained or analyzed a given thesis, hypothesis, sub-field, artifact or the like that the researcher will focus on. Even in a short two-page research paper, it is necessary to explain the significance of the secondary sources you used in your analysis and how your findings build on top of the gaps they left out.

Modes of Discourse

Three major modes of discourse are involved in a standard research paper. You have to summarize or describe the artifact you are researching. Then, you have to analyze the evidence, linking it together into groupings, explaining its significance, and deriving conclusions from it. Lastly, all research papers are tied together with a single coherent argument, thesis or hypothesis that they set out to prove.

Description: There are many types of description, including descriptions of how characters or settings look and narration of the plotline in a fiction or non-fiction story in the artifact. Firstly, these descriptions should introduce readers unfamiliar with a given artifact to its contents. Secondly, great descriptions should also present the relevant details that help you prove your argument. If you are considering a work from an economic perspective, the narrative should stress the parts of a book or film that are related to money, jobs and other economy-related components. On the other hand, if you are writing about aesthetics, the descriptions should be of how the actors or characters in the artifact look, as well as other beauty-related components. It is problematic when there are too few of these descriptions and when they are too lengthy and offer irrelevant information.

Exposition: Analysis is an interpretation of the facts or evidence. This analysis centers on the opinions the writer arrives at as he or she based on the evidence. The evidence in a primary source alone can be sufficient to base your own opinions on in some scientific fields. In the field of literary or cultural studies analysis, experts' opinions are necessary because proving an argument about fiction involves too many abstract speculations. In other words, in a concrete scientific experiment on the effects of consuming a given chemical in rats, the findings will point to obvious conclusions based on the statistical results. It would not be necessary to use other similar experiments to support the argument, if the findings are definitive as a large number of rats were studied for a long period of time in a controlled and unbiased study. On the other hand, a fiction book is inherently untrue as all fiction is a series of fabricated lies. The text might be final, but interpretations of the same event can vary widely. For example, if Charles Dickens' *A Tale of Two Cities* ends with the victory of the French revolutionaries, does this mean that Dickens supports or opposes the French Revolution? Literary researchers disagree on this point as they do on most other points that involve fiction. Thus, if you are going to join an ongoing debate on a point such as this, you are expected to use secondary sources that share your opinions to support the likelihood of truthfulness in your own. If you use secondary opinions, you are being assisted in your analysis by the research conducted by these sources.

Argument: The argument is the glue that connects the evidence with your opinions and stresses that your analysis is correct and truthful. An earlier section of this book looked at the components of a logical argument, and future sections will explore it in more depth. For now, examples of successful arguments related to the political and economic terms required for Essay 2 should help to explain what all strong arguments have in common. Nicolo Machiavelli's *The Prince*, based on the Italian monarchy, is still a popular philosophy textbook even though it was published in 1532. It is based on much earlier philosophies such as Plato's *Republic* (380BC), about ancient Greece, which established the Socratic argumentative method that uses logic to build arguments by proving that if something is true, something related to it is likely to also be true. Both *The Prince* and the *Republic* attempt to explain the governmental systems that the authors saw practiced in the states that they resided in, and attempts are made to explain how these systems can be improved to benefit the members of these societies. Machiavelli wrote *The Prince* with the hope that he could educate his own soon-to-be-king to become a better ruler, but he ended up spending many years in prison for conspiracy against the Medici family via his radical military strategies as a general and outspoken opinions in his writings. The opening part of the quote below is frequently used in other great philosophical and political textbooks that have been written after this work. This is a great example of the use of logic to derive a conclusion. He uses powerful examples and impactful analogies to explain his opinions. Studying the structure of this argument can help any writer become a stronger debater.

The second segment is from Thomas Paine's *Rights of Man*. This work contributed to defending Americans victory in the Revolutionary War and their fight not only against British oppression but also the monarchical style of government. Because the Founding Fathers were proponents of democracy, this is a key source for understanding the democratic ideals that were at the source of the revolutionary movement. Referenced in this piece, Edmund Burke's *Reflections on the Revolution in France* was published in 1790, a year before Paine's criticism. The French Revolution took place between 1789 and 1799, and its outcome was far from certain when both of these works were written. The American Revolution actually started before the one in France and lasted between 1765 and 1783. Paine's earlier treatise, *Common Sense*, made a stronger impact on rousing Americans into battle in the heat of the Revolution in 1776. When it comes to Paine's *Rights of Man* and Burke's *Revolution*, both are still significant philosophical works, but Burke fell on the wrong side of history, so he is slightly less familiar to American readers. Burke's analysis criticized the revolutionaries in France for their violent actions, while Paine argues for a violent revolution as the only logical course of action against a tyrannical, monarchical power.

In the same year when Paine published *Common Sense*, 1776, Adam Smith released *An Inquiry into the Nature and Causes of the Wealth of Nations*. One of the reasons the American and Revolutions could be funded was because of the growth of the merchant and capitalist class in these countries. Prior to this point, only aristocrats and monarchs could amass enough funds in taxation to initiate wars. So Smith is really examining the wealth of capitalists rather than the wealth of the monarchs that were the predominant rules of nations at the times when this work was composed. There is a great deal to learn from Smith's argument in this work, starting with the fact that he includes a variation on the two terms familiar to most arguments, cause and effect, in the title.

The last of these works was released a century later during the 1848 Revolutions in Europe. *The Communist Manifesto* is attributed primarily to Karl Marx in casual conversations, but he wrote it with his writing partner, Friedrich Engels. They were asked to write this declaration to propagandize their cause to potential fighters in their active revolution in Germany, just as Paine was commissioned to write *Common Sense* for the American Revolution. This particular section is significant because it defines what communism is from the pen of its primary founders. There are more repetitions of the term "communists" and what they stand for than would be appropriate for an average research paper, but this part of the work is the logical deduction or argument that arrives at conclusions based on the relationship between true claims. Other sections of the manifesto present the narrative of historical truths and other evidence that supports these conclusions.

If you are covering one of these terms in your essay, you should utilize short quotes or summaries of these works to enrich your arguments about cultural artifacts. There are plenty of other books written in support of these political and cultural movements, but these are the best-known and most frequently employed in derivative research.

Totalitarianism: From Nicolo Machiavelli's *The Prince*, "Chapter XVII—Concerning Cruelty and Clemency, and Whether It Is Better to Be Loved than Feared"

Upon this a question arises: whether it be better to be loved than feared or feared than loved? It may be answered that one should wish to be both, but, because it is difficult to unite them in one person, it is much safer to be feared than loved, when, of the two, either must be dispensed with. Because this is to be asserted in general of men, that they are ungrateful, fickle, false, cowardly, covetous, and as long as you succeed they are yours entirely; they will offer you their blood, property, life, and children, as is said above, when the need is far distant; but when it approaches they turn against you. And that prince who, relying entirely on their promises, has neglected other precautions, is ruined; because friendships that are obtained by payments, and not by greatness or nobility of mind, may indeed be earned, but they are not secured, and in time of need cannot be relied upon; and men have less scruple in offending one who is beloved than one who is feared, for love is preserved by the link of obligation which, owing to the baseness of men, is broken at every opportunity for their advantage; but fear preserves you by a dread of punishment which never fails.

Nevertheless a prince ought to inspire fear in such a way that, if he does not win love, he avoids hatred; because he can endure very well being feared whilst he is not hated, which will always be as long as he abstains from the property of his citizens and subjects and from their women. But when it is necessary for him to proceed against the life of someone, he must do it on proper justification and for manifest cause, but above all things he must keep his hands off the property of others, because men more quickly forget the death of their father than the loss of their patrimony. Besides, pretexts for taking away the property are never wanting; for he who has once begun to live by robbery will always find pretexts for seizing what belongs to others; but reasons for taking life, on the contrary, are more difficult to find and sooner lapse. But when a prince is with his army, and has under control a multitude of soldiers, then it is quite necessary for him to disregard the reputation of cruelty, for without it he would never hold his army united or disposed to its duties.

Democracy: From Thomas Paine's *Rights of Man: The Writings of Thomas Paine, Volume II*, "Chapter III. Of the Old and New Systems of Government":

> Though the ancient governments present to us a miserable picture of the condition of man, there is one which above all others exempts itself from the general description. I mean the democracy of the Athenians. We see more to admire, and less to condemn, in that great, extraordinary people, than in anything which history affords.
>
> Mr. Burke is so little acquainted with constituent principles of government, that he confounds democracy and representation together. Representation was a thing unknown in the ancient democracies. In those the mass of the people met and enacted laws (grammatically speaking) in the first person. Simple democracy was no other than the common hall of the ancients. It signifies the form, as well as the public principle of the government. As those democracies increased in population, and the territory extended, the simple democratical form became unwieldy and impracticable; and as the system of representation was not known, the consequence was, they either degenerated convulsively into monarchies, or became absorbed into such as then existed. Had the system of representation been then understood, as it now is, there is no reason to believe that those forms of government, now called monarchical or aristocratical, would ever have taken place. It was the want of some method to consolidate the parts of society, after it became too populous, and too extensive for the simple democratical form, and also the lax and solitary condition of shepherds and herdsmen in other parts of the world, that afforded opportunities to those unnatural modes of government to begin.

Capitalism: From Adam Smith's *An Inquiry into the Nature and Causes of the Wealth of Nations*, "Chapter I. Of the Division of Labour":

> The greatest improvements in the productive powers of labour, and the greater part of the skill, dexterity, and judgment, with which it is anywhere directed, or applied, seem to have been the effects of the division of labour. The effects of the division of labour, in the general business of society, will be more easily understood, by considering in what manner it operates in some particular manufactures. It is commonly supposed to be carried furthest in some very trifling ones; not perhaps that it really is carried further in them than in others of more importance: but in those trifling manufac-

tures which are destined to supply the small wants of but a small number of people, the whole number of workmen must necessarily be small; and those employed in every different branch of the work can often be collected into the same workhouse, and placed at once under the view of the spectator.

In those great manufactures, on the contrary, which are destined to supply the great wants of the great body of the people, every different branch of the work employs so great a number of workmen, that it is impossible to collect them all into the same workhouse. We can seldom see more, at one time, than those employed in one single branch. Though in such manufactures, therefore, the work may really be divided into a much greater number of parts, than in those of a more trifling nature, the division is not near so obvious, and has accordingly been much less observed.

To take an example, therefore, from a very trifling manufacture, but one in which the division of labour has been very often taken notice of, the trade of a pin-maker: a workman not educated to this business (which the division of labour has rendered a distinct trade), nor acquainted with the use of the machinery employed in it (to the invention of which the same division of labour has probably given occasion), could scarce, perhaps, with his utmost industry, make one pin in a day, and certainly could not make twenty. But in the way in which this business is now carried on, not only the whole work is a peculiar trade, but it is divided into a number of branches, of which the greater part are likewise peculiar trades. One man draws out the wire; another straights it; a third cuts it; a fourth points it; a fifth grinds it at the top for receiving the head; to make the head requires two or three distinct operations; to put it on is a peculiar business; to whiten the pins is another; it is even a trade by itself to put them into the paper; and the important business of making a pin is, in this manner, divided into about eighteen distinct operations, which, in some manufactories, are all performed by distinct hands, though in others the same man will sometimes perform two or three of them. I have seen a small manufactory of this kind, where ten men only were employed, and where some of them consequently performed two or three distinct operations. But though they were very poor, and therefore but indifferently accommodated with the necessary machinery, they could, when they exerted themselves, make among them about twelve pounds of pins in a day. There are in a pound upwards of four thousand pins of a middling size. Those ten persons, therefore, could make among them upwards of forty-eight thousand pins in a day. Each person, therefore, making a tenth part of forty-eight thousand pins, might be considered as making four thousand eight hundred pins in a day. But if they had all wrought separately and independently, and without any of them having been educated to this peculiar business, they certainly could not each of them have made twenty, perhaps not one pin in a day; that is, certainly, not the two hundred and fortieth, perhaps not the four thousand eight hundredth, part of what they are at present capable of performing, in consequence of a proper division and combination of their different operations.

Communism and Socialism: From Karl Marx and Friedrich Engels' *The Communist Manifesto*, "II. Proletarians and Communists":

In what relation do the Communists stand to the proletarians as a whole?

The Communists do not form a separate party opposed to other working-class parties.

They have no interests separate and apart from those of the proletariat as a whole.

They do not set up any sectarian principles of their own, by which to shape and mould the proletarian movement.

The Communists are distinguished from the other working-class parties by this only: (1) In the national struggles of the proletarians of the different countries, they point out and bring to the front the common interests of the entire proletariat, independently of all nationality. (2) In the various stages of development which the struggle of the working class against the bourgeoisie has to pass through, they always and everywhere represent the interests of the movement as a whole.

The Communists, therefore, are on the one hand, practically, the most advanced and resolute section of the working-class parties of every country, that section which pushes forward all others; on the other hand, theoretically, they have over the great mass of the proletariat the advantage of clearly understanding the line of march, the conditions, and the ultimate general results of the proletarian movement.

The immediate aim of the Communist is the same as that of all the other proletarian parties: formation of the proletariat into a class, overthrow of the bourgeois supremacy, conquest of political power by the proletariat.

The theoretical conclusions of the Communists are in no way based on ideas or principles that have been invented, or discovered, by this or that would-be universal reformer. They merely express, in general terms, actual relations springing from an existing class struggle, from a historical movement going on under our very eyes. The abolition of existing property relations is not at all a distinctive feature of Communism.

All property relations in the past have continually been subject to historical change consequent upon the change in historical conditions.

The French Revolution, for example, abolished feudal property in favour of bourgeois property.

The distinguishing feature of Communism is not the abolition of property generally, but the abolition of bourgeois property. But modern bourgeois private property is the final and most complete expression of the system of producing and appropriating products, that is based on class antagonisms, on the exploitation of the many by the few.

In this sense, the theory of the Communists may be summed up in the single sentence: Abolition of private property.

Organization

A research paper can also be broken down into these components: background, purpose, evidence, analysis, and conclusions. Thus, unlike some other essay types, that can have merely an introduction, body and conclusion, the background, purpose, evidence and analysis are essential components without which no research paper can be complete. Background is composed of a narrative that summarizes a cultural artifact, or it can be a literature review of past findings on the subject. The purpose for the study should be mentioned, even if only briefly to avoid leaving the reader unsure why this particular argument is significant. And obviously, it is not a research paper if there is no evidence presented or analyzed. The essential components of a research paper's organization can also be divided into: claim, support and warrant.

Claims: Each claim is a mini-thesis that proposes that a component of your argument is truthful, valuable or helpful. Claims can be divided into three sub-categories: propositions of fact, value or policy.

fact = truth

When you set out to proposition that you are offering factual information, you are arguing that these details are truthful. Examples of factual evidence include testimonies from witnesses, interviews with primary sources, and statistics on the narrow subject. Facts can also be proven with reference or primary and secondary source materials.

value = judgments

The proposition of value is a claim that relies on a judgement of a given position. While some arguments are correct simply because they can be proven to be statistically factual, most political and economic arguments rely on appeals to the reader's values. These value-based claims might attempt to persuade readers to approve or disapprove on a newly proposed policy, ideology or idea. The ideology in question might be broad, such as communism or capitalism as a system. A policy might be very narrow, such as the addition of a new stoplight at a specific intersection. The claim of value might also be in support of a particular mass or individual action. It can argue on behalf of a belief in terms of if it is right or wrong, or possibly if it is worthwhile or unnecessary. When you engage in arguments that touch on values, you want to make sure that you use examples to make abstract values more grounded in facts. In other words, avoid simply saying that one set of values is better than another set, and instead support this value claim with factual claims as well.

policy = actions

Claims of policy combine value judgements with factual evidence to propagandize for certain actions or policies. The policy supported should typically be stated in the Thesis or in the topic sentence that uses utilizes this type of a claim. Usually, these claims differ from other value arguments because they include a proposal for a solution to the central problem being examined, or a statement of what needs to change in the current system.

Support: As was explained earlier, the supportive evidence are the primary and secondary sources that support the claims with verifiable facts.

Warrant: The glue between claims and evidence is a warrant. Warrants explain the reliability of the secondary sources that are presented in support of the argument. Warrants can also explain that there is a clear relationship between the claim and the supporting evidence. In other words, if you fail to link the evidence with your opinions by explaining their relationship, the argument will fall apart. In most essays, a few well-placed words can explain this relationship, so that the presence of the warrant is not obvious to the reader. The warrant is simply a logical link in the chain, similar to a transition, rather than an element that receives a leading position in the text in terms of words devoted to it. Some lengthier warrants set out to prove that secondary sources utilized are authoritative, or that they are reliable. Mentioning that the source comes from a reputable journal because it is published by Harvard University Press might be sufficient, but you might need to dive deeper into this examination of the sources' reputation or substance if it has been questioned by some of the other scholars you have reviewed. Some warrants make a link by attempting to motivate readers and explaining the relationship via preferred values or needs of the audience.

Works Cited

Marx, Karl and Friedrich Engels. "II. Proletarians and Communists." *The Communist Manifesto*. 25 January 2005. Project Gutenberg. 30 September 2016. Web.

Machiavelli, Nicolo. "Chapter XVII—Concerning Cruelty and Clemency, and Whether It Is Better to Be Loved than Feared." *The Prince*. 26 August 2016. Project Gutenberg. 30 September 2016. Web.

Paine, Thomas. "Chapter III. Of the Old and New Systems of Government." *Rights of Man. The Writings of Thomas Paine, Volume II*. 15 November 2012. Project Gutenberg. 30 September 2016. Web.

Smith, Adam. "Chapter I. Of the Division of Labour." *An Inquiry into the Nature and Causes of the Wealth of Nations*. 5 June 2011. Project Gutenberg. 30 September 2016. Web.

Part 6

Formatting and Writing Essays on a Computer

This is a technical section that explains how to format and otherwise write an essay on a computer. This information is essential because a vast majority of students make these types of formatting mistakes. They frequently have never written a research paper before, nor have they taken a computer class, so corrections in this area are always practically useful. In future classes, they might be asked to double or single space an essay, so they have to learn how to do this an introductory research writing class like this one (rather than later, when points might be subtracted from their grade for these mistakes). Students also need to know how to indent paragraphs, how to change fonts, and how to insert charts, pictures and tables. Students also frequently mistake quotation marks with italics, so there's a section that explains when it's appropriate to use one or the other. Adding footnotes and symbols can also cause difficulty. The Thesaurus is a useful tool in Word that allows a student to quickly check the meaning of an unfamiliar word or to find synonyms or antonyms to diversify their vocabulary. The Track Changes feature is especially useful in group writing assignments, or when students go to a Writing Center for assistance. From this discussion, the book moves into a Group Writing Assignment, and then the Ethnicity Essay Assignment. The first asks for students to read about and discuss the topic of Border Wall construction and then jointly write an essay for or against it. The Ethnicity Essay asks students to criticize a cultural artifact (film or book) in terms of how it approaches ethnicity: for example, if its accepting of different ethnic groups or discriminatory. Professors can adjust these or other components to their particular classes. Since UTRGV is on the Mexican-American border, the Border Wall topic is particularly relevant for this region. Instructors are encouraged to find articles on topics that fit ethnic or other tensions common in their geographical area.

Gender Bias Essay Assignment

Write a 2-Page Essay that addresses the topic of gender in the American or another world culture. The essay should examine a specific cultural artifact. If you are uncertain about what type of an artifact would work, simply write about a fictional novel or feature film. It will be easier for you to compose this essay if you choose an artifact with a particularly strong message about gender, either because it is ultra-conventional or ultra-radical and innovative. If gender plays a central role in the artifact, it will be easier for you to find evidence to make a researched argument about it. Similarly to the Politics/Economics Essay, this essay will be graded based on:

- the presence of a narrative of the plotline/ story depicted in the artifact
- the use of two secondary sources related to the artifact or gender studies in addition to the primary artifact
- a central cohesive argument that relates the concept of "gender" to the artifact
- a clear writing style that is readable and lacks major errors
- participation in the Editing Workshop

Try to avoid making a biased argument and instead evaluate potentially biased or unique perspectives on gender with the detachment of a professional researcher. Your job is not to criticize or judge gender role assignment, but rather to try to see gender from a distant perspective. We are inundated with messages about what men and women typically do and most of these are simply biases rather than scientific facts. If you step outside of your own biases about gender to evaluate somebody else's it should help you to better understand the culture around us. As with the other essays, avoid bringing in your own personal experiences, and instead focus on what established scholars in the field of gender studies have said about your narrow topic or a related field. Most of our interpersonal relationships change depending on the gender of the person we are communicating with, so giving some thought to what gender means, what it is, how it is influenced and the like should help all of us to improve our relationships with both genders and with those who cross between them.

As you move forward in your academic studies and later enter the work-world, there are some functions in Word that will help you to bring a polished message across. If you follow these standards, your work will make a great first impression on your professors and employers. These rules are similar to wearing a suit and tie to an interview. They might not be required, but they can give you a boost over the competition. If your essay is missing necessary components, it will look disheveled even if it contains superior content.

Double-Spacing versus Single-Spacing

You can change the spacing from double to single space in the paragraph screen, numbered (1) in this image. Spacing requirements differ based on the type of text you are writing. Scholarly or college essays typically require double-spacing, or for there to be lines skipped automatically between all of the paragraphs. You should not hit "Enter" between these paragraphs, but rather choose the Double spacing option on this screen. If you hit "Enter" between the lines, Word will not be able to check the fragments for grammatical errors and it might insert capitalization where it is not needed. Single spacing is used in business communications, where you want to save paper and communicate the message succinctly. The Double spacing allows for a professor or another reviewer to insert comments in the margins between the lines. Some memos and emails also have blank spaces between paragraphs, rather than between each of the lines. The spaces are only insert between paragraphs when it is difficult to indent the paragraphs otherwise, such as in email programs that do not allow for such tabbing. So, you should ask your supervisor or professor about any spacing re-

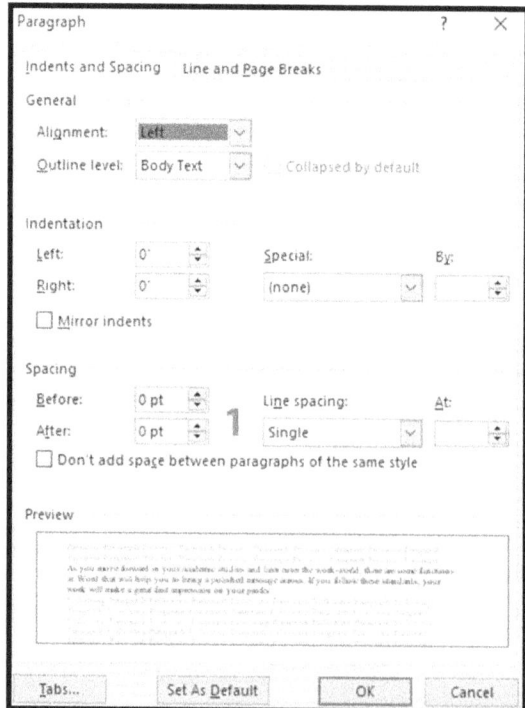

quirements, and then follow these guidelines.

Paragraph Indentation

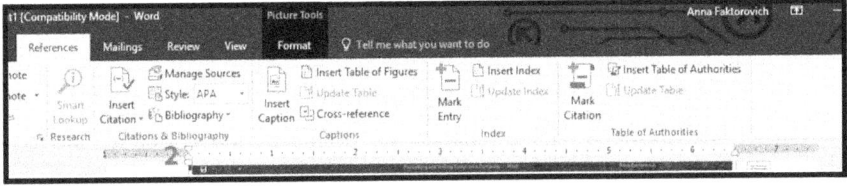

Paragraph indentation is necessary to separate ideas into sub-categories. Without clear indentations at the start of new paragraphs, readers will not be able to tell when you move on from one topic to the next. A typical 2-page essay should have five paragraphs. If you merge the text together into a single, long paragraph, your ideas will also be convoluted or compacted together. The paragraph breaks help to explain how your ideas are categorized and organized. One paragraph might be narrating the plotline, while three other paragraphs might be offering three supporting arguments. The tabs explain this separation even if you do not have clear transitions between them. The best way to change indentations in your paragraphs is with the ruler, shown in image (2) above.

To indent a **regular paragraph**, such as this one, move the top part of the hourglass at the start of the white portion of the ruler over to the desired indentation level. Most college essays should be indented by .5". Books, including this one, are typically indented by .25" because they have a smaller page width. Larger indentations than .5" are pretty uncommon unless you're using a page size larger than the standard 8.5" width.

Works Cited entries are typically indented in a backwards pattern, so that the first line of the entry is not indented, while those that follow it are indented by a set width. Here is one such example from an earlier chapter:

Marx, Karl and Friedrich Engels. "II. Proletarians and Communists." *The Communist Manifesto*. 25 January 2005. Project Gutenberg. 30 September 2016. Web.

As you can see, this is the reverse from the rest of this paragraph. This is done so that the last names of the authors stand out, and it is easier to find a specific entry if it is a long list. Thus, definitely remember to create this reverse indentation in longer research papers. To do this, move the bottom part of the cone on the ruler over by .5" (in a research paper), while keeping the top at the start of the white portion of the ruler. You should place the hourglass on the line where you plan on entering the indented text, or select the lines or paragraphs of the text you want to indent before moving the hourglass.

Long quotations, or those over 4 lines in length, should be separated from the text with a colon, like the one above, or a sentence that introduces this text. These blocks of text should have all of their lines indented by .5" rather than only the first or the following lines. To do this, you would move the whole hourglass (top and bottom) over by .5", after selecting the text. Lines out of a poem or lyrics are also separated this way:

> Here is what these lines look like
> When they are indented.

Fonts

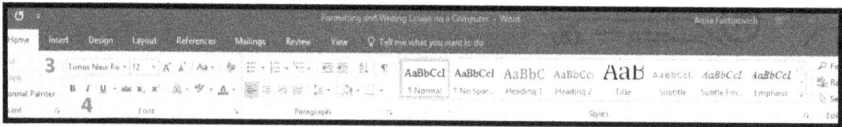

The most common font used in college essays is Times New Roman, as shown in (3) above. The standard font size is 12 pt. Especially when you are submitting an essay through an online system, such as Blackboard, you should not use a smaller font than 12 pt. because those systems are standardized and the font will look a lot smaller than it would appear on your screen at 100% zoom. At the same time, you should not use larger fonts, such as 14 pt. and up, because these make it look as if you wanted to do less work and so you attempted to fill the required 2 pages with giant letters instead of following the implied rules of the assignment. Most scholarly books, including this one, use the Garamond font, or more specifically the more widely available Adobe Garamond Pro font. There are many other common fonts that are acceptable for academic writing as long as they are not too FLASHY. If you are doing a creative assignment, you can find many innovative fonts in the free Google Fonts collection, but it would take some effort to properly download and utilize these on your home computer.

Italics, Quotations, Bold or Underlines

In the same screen shot as (3), you can also see the portion of the Home tab that can *italicize* (*I*), **bold** (**B**) or underline (U) text (4). Underlines were used instead of italics back when office work was conducted on typewriters, and these machines could underline, but could not change the entire letter style with italics. With modern computing, italics became the standard way to separate title of books, feature films and various other materials. Bold is typically used in titles, or when you want to stress a word in the text as particularly significant. Though, only college textbooks and some other genres use bold for stress, while in college essays and other genres, italics are more commonly used for this purpose. Another alternative is placing quotation marks around the significant text. Quotations are obviously used when you want to quote from a primary or a secondary source without your essay. Quotations are also used when you want to signify that something is a short work, such as an essay or a chapter out of a book, or a short film. For example, this section is called, "Italics, Quotations, Bold or Underlines." It is a common mistake to confuse the types of content that should be italicized versus the type that is placed in quotations, so if you are unsure, you should look it up on the *MLA Handbook* before proceeding.

Charts

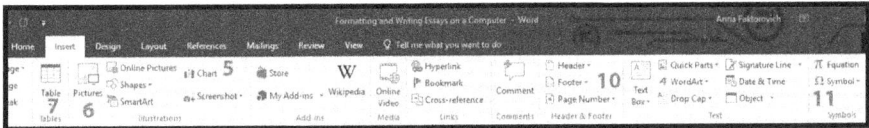

Charts are useful when you want to visually represent your own or another party's statistical findings or other numeric data. Listing the statistics as pure numbers might not be as easy to grasp for the reader as seeing the same data represented in a chart. The difference between peaks and lows is immediately apparent. Charts are frequently used in business presentations and in other professional settings. So, if you plan on including statistics in any of your college papers, you might want to insert a chart as well. When you click on (5) above to create a chart in Word, an Excel table will appear. When you enter your data into this table, a chart the represents these numbers will be automatically created for you in Word. There are many different charts you can create including pie charts, and very basic graphs with two peaks. The chart below is a more complex example, if you need to compare several levels of data.

Chart Title

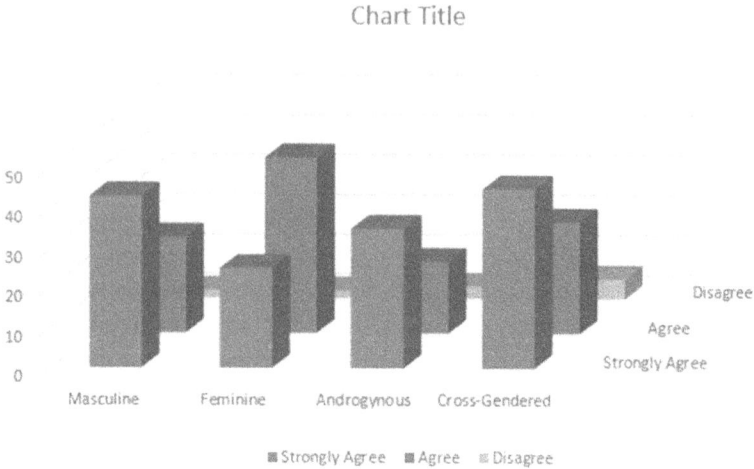

Pictures

Item (6) in the diagram above, on the Insert tab, can be used to insert a picture into your essay. Pictures are particularly useful when you are writing an essay about a visual art, such as about a feature film. If you are watching the film on Netflix or another digital format, you can press the "PrntScr" button on your computer's keyboard to clip a shot out of the movie that represent your argument as a strong supporting evidence. You can also use the "Screenshot" option on the "Insert" tab, right under the "Chart" option, to make this image right in Word.

Figure 1. *Hotel Transylvania 2*

As you can see above, when you insert a still from a film, you should insert the name of the film and a number for the image, in case you have more than one.

Tables

The Insert tab also allows you to create a "Table" (7). If you have a great deal of detailed or complex data, it is easier to summarize it in a table rather than using a chart. In these cases, having too many spikes on the chart, would make them difficult to interpret.

Plotlines	Stage 1	Stage 2	Stage 3	Stage 4
Movie A	X	A	U	W
Movie B	Y	X	H	R
Movie C	Z	C	N	D
Movie D	G	V	M	G
Movie E	E	B	B	H

Inserting Automatic Parts

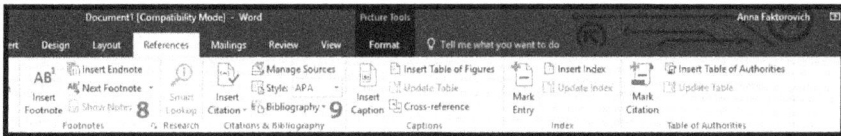

There are several options in Word that allow you to create pretty complex research paper components with pretty simple clicks. **Footnotes** (8) are used when you want to insert a comment about where some of the information you are providing comes from, or if you want to add details to the argument that are a tangent, or unrelated to your central argument. Some authors also place their in-text citations into footnotes. There are several complex rules that apply to the creation of footnotes that you should research before you apply them to a lengthy research project. But, if you simply need to insert a general footnote, you should be aware of where in Word these are generated.

You can generate a **citation** (9) in Word too. If you are unsure about the style you should use to create an MLA, APA or another citation type, you can click on "Insert Citation," and then the screen included below will appear. For the papers in this class, you should select the MLA style before opening this window. Then, you should choose the type of material you plan on creating an entry for, such as "Book" or "Journal Article." Then, you enter the rest of the information and click "OK" and an entry will be created with proper italics, and quotation and punctuation marks. But, you have to properly capitalize the title and reverse name the author yourself. First an in-text citation for the book without the page number will appear. Then, you have to click on "Bibliography" to see the full entry that you can use in your essay.

Footers

The diagram in the "Charts" section included an option to add **page numbers** (10). Numbering the pages only becomes necessary in longer research papers. You should not number pages if an essay is only 2-3 pages long. They are usually required when a long research paper is printed out, in case the papers separate and have to be put back into the correct order. The quick way to insert numbers is on the "Insert" tab, where you can select "Page Number" and then select the position where you want it to appear. Alternatively, you can select "Footer," and then add your **last name** and/or paper **title** together with the page number in the footer. The name and title are only necessary in very formal and very long research papers.

Symbols

If you are writing a paper on foreign cultures or economics, or other unique topics, you might occasionally need to use symbols to add to your text. These are available on the "Insert" tab (11). Some of these symbols are: the symbol for the British pound £, copyrights sign ©, and the not equal to sign ≠. Knowing where these are can save you some frustration if you suddenly need to find them later down the line.

Thesaurus

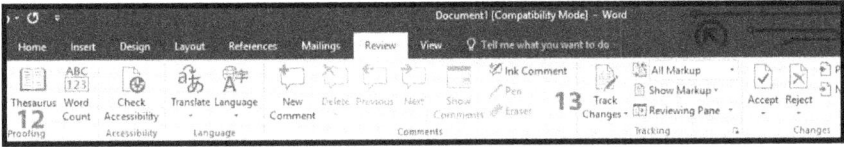

As I mentioned in an earlier section, the Thesaurus feature (12) can be very helpful in looking up the basic meaning of a word you are thinking about using. To use it, you should select the word you are unsure about, and then click on "Thesaurus" on the "Review" tab. A list of synonyms will appear. If the synonyms sound like the word you were hoping to use, you can proceed, and if not, you can search for a few alternative words until you find the word that reflects your intended meaning.

Track Changes

The "Review" tab also allows you to turn on the "Track Changes" (13) option. Once selected, any edits you make to the essay will be highlighted and saved together with the original version of your essay, so that you can go back and look over the changes to select those you want to keep and those you want to reject. This is usually used in editing workshops or when somebody else is proofreading your essay. But, it can also help you as you edit, if you might otherwise delete something unintentionally.

Group Writing Assignment

Write a Letter to the Future President Presenting Your Argument on the Mexican-US Border Wall

Step 1: Read the article or a portion of the article you were assigned aloud for the group.

Step 2: Take a vote on if the members of your group in response to this question:

Should a wall be completed across the entire Mexican-US border?
    Agree
    Disagree

Step 3: Elect one of the team members to jot down the key points you bring up for or against the wall. Have a brief general discussion with the group about this question and why the members agree or disagree with this question. During the discussion, you can use the arguments offered in the article, or bring in your own ideas.

Step 4: Continue the discussion by looking closely at the key points you've written down, are they arguments about facts or truthfulness, or are they arguments about values, beliefs, or assumptions? Do you think racism is one of the "beliefs" at play in this debate? Considering that the article states that illegal immigration has been on a decline since the start of the Great Recession, why do you think Trump brought this particular issue into the debate (i.e.: is he indirectly implying that Hillary is inferior to him because she is a woman, as he is undervaluing Hispanic immigrants)?

Step 5: Assign (via a vote) the following components to the members in your group (if it's a small group, each might do more than one component):

- **Summarize** the position on this issue that the majority of your group supports
- **Write a paragraph** on one of the **key points** you agreed on (can be attempted by 3+ members)

- **Write a paragraph** that focuses on the **racist "beliefs"** question
- If one of your group members **disagreed** with others, they should write a **paragraph** that explains this **alternative position** in a way that blends with the rest of the argument
- **Write** a few **concluding sentences** wherein you make a **request for change on this issue** to the Future President
- **Read** the paper to the rest of the class after **editing** it to make sure it is cohesive and makes sense as a whole

Reflection Writing Exercise:

Write a 500-word reflection on the group border writing project. This assignment will be submitted as evidence in an assessment of Team Work in 1305 classes across UTRGV. It will count as class work, rather than as a regular short essay. You do not need to do any research for it. You just have to reflect on your group experience with this exercise. Include the following components in your cohesive essay reflection:

- Summarize what happened in your group and the exercise.
- Describe the role you played in the team, or what you contributed to this project. Were you elected to play this role? Did you choose it? Were you happy with playing this role versus another one? Do you think you made a constructive positive contribution to the outcome for your team?
- Were the members of your team in agreement on the central question you were tackling? Were there some disagreements about the supporting points the group ended up making? How did you resolve these disagreements, if/ when they came up? Were there any negative, unsolvable problems that went with facing these disagreements, or were they all resolved and handled in a positive way that benefited the group? How so?
- Do you think you were more productive working in a group rather than in an individual writing assignment? Did the team dynamic help you achieve your joined mission? Were there any difficulties in moving forward or deciding on how to proceed because it was a group effort? Can you suggest how the team dynamic might have been improved if you could re-do this exercise?
- What can you tell students who are about to engage in a group writing activity that might help them succeed? What strategies, techniques or interpersonal communications might help them

work better in a team setting?

Submit this reflection to the Wall Group Reflection assignment section in Blackboard by the listed due date.

Ethnicity Essay Assignment

Write a 2-Page Essay that addresses the topic of ethnicity in a world culture. The essay should examine a specific cultural artifact (probably a fictional book or film). Ethnicity plays a major role in world politics as it moves countries towards wars and inspires uprisings of a minor ethnic group against the majority or the reverse. The readings due during this section contain some approaches on how ethnicity can be researched and argued about. Once again, the essay will be graded on:

- the presence of a narrative of the plotline or story depicted in the artifact
- the use of two secondary, scholarly sources (preferably found through the UTRGV Library website) related to the artifact or ethnicity studies, (in addition to the primary artifact)
- a central cohesive argument that relates the concept of "ethnicity" to the artifact
- a clear writing style that is readable and lacks major errors
- participation in the Editing Workshop (10%)

Modern popular culture is saturated in ridicule of outside cultures and a propaganda for itself. Middle Eastern, Asian, Mexican and other cultural groups are seen as the "other" and are depicted with unkind stereotypes. There is a perceived post-racial state, while the media perpetuates biases against ethnic groups. For this essay, you should look closely at one of these depictions to evaluate it for racism or for fair and appropriate display of a unique ethnicity. This category looks at anything from clothing, to language, to dialect, to manners and to dance styles, so there are many possible approaches to this project.

Part 7

Elements of Research

This part dives more in depth into the elements of research and research writing. It offers information on proper in text and bibliographic or Works Cited book and parts of a book citations. The section on plagiarism and academic integrity might be covered in the first week of class by more cautious instructors. Plagiarism is a huge problem in academia, and this section explains why this is the case in the hope of stopping students from making this mistake. The final section explains how information from multiple sources can be synthesized into a single, coherent research paper.

MLA Book and Part of a Book Citations

Research papers nearly always included a Works Cited list. It is impossible to perform serious research without building it on the research of previous scholars. This applies to scientific studies and to literary analysis. Without Einstein and Galileo's theories, scientists today would have to prove their theorems before proceeding to propose new additions or directions. Learning to rely on secondary sources to strengthen your argument is an important part of becoming a serious researcher, and to advancing in your academic studies. Citing these sources properly is a way of crediting these helpful authors, similarly to how you would thank your producer and director at an Academy Awards speech. There are very specific rules about properly citing sources. These rules exist so that future researchers can understand the shorthand you are employing and find the exact sources, page numbers and the like to reproduce your research if they plan on taking it a step further. If you are lucky, perhaps one of your sources might be of special relevance to this future researcher. Still, even if nobody double-checks your sources, proper citations show your knowledge of the research craft, so that your work appears to be professionally done.

This section is divided only into a sub-section on "books" and another on "parts of books" because there are two significantly different styles for citing items in an MLA Works Cited list. All long works or entire projects are cited in the same style as books. All relatively short works are cited in the style of a segment.

Books

If you have inserted a book title or a feature film name into your essay, you should be familiar that all of these are italicized. For example, you would write *A Tale of Two Cities* or *Harry Potter*. To create an entry for the first of these, I looked it up on Project Gutenberg. This source of texts is great for free, public domain, digital editions of world classics in fiction and nonfiction. The "public domain" currently includes any work published before 1923 in any country. Some books published after this date might also be in the public domain but you would have to research their qualifications. Gutenberg has scanned a large volume of these great early books and then translated them into html texts. It is very easy to grab quotes and to search for key words in these versions, so I use them frequently in my research.

To start the citation, I usually write the author's name in the reverse, as you would do for the musician in a music video. I attempt this below. Then, you should double-check the full name of the book's title. In this case, there is a subtitle in addition to the name it is well-known for, *A Tale of Two Cities: A Story of the French Revolution*. Then, I usually run into a glitch with Gutenberg, as they usually fail to scan in the copyrights page with the information about the location and name of the publisher and the year of publication. If you Google the book, this information is easy to find for all classics, and it turns out that the first edition was published in 1859 by Chapman & Hall in London. Even though this is a digital book, I prefer to enter this information as well to give credit to the original publisher that is being transcribed. Some other sources that explain MLA citations, suggest that you only put the original year of publication in parenthesis after the title, as in: (1859). And others recommend not including the name of the city of publication as you would with a print publication. And yet others, skip the publisher, year and city all together because Gutenberg is not including these. So, I am including some variations below, all of which are appropriate. The last entry is the formula for the second version, which is probably the best one. You should only use the first entry if you are using a physical book, as otherwise you will not have the physical page numbers to insert into your in-text citations. The confusion in proper citation style is due in part to the numerous releases of new versions of the *MLA Handbook* (now in its 8th 2016 edition), and the constant changes in digital publishing. Some instructors are more discerning about the style, and are likely to subtract points if you forget any one of the required parts or bits of punctuation. So, you should inquire regarding your professors' MLA style preferences. Including the components that you can easily find in the sources is usually acceptable, and only rarely do you want to do additional research to include a "full" citation.

Works Cited

Dickens, Charles. *A Tale of Two Cities: A Story of the French Revolution*. London: Chapman & Hall, 1859. Print.

Dickens, Charles. *A Tale of Two Cities: A Story of the French Revolution*. Chapman & Hall, 1859. Project Gutenberg. Web. 5 November 2016.

Dickens, Charles. *A Tale of Two Cities: A Story of the French Revolution.*
(1859). Project Gutenberg. Web. 5 Nov 2016.
Last Name, First. *Title: Subtitle.* Publisher, Year of Original Publication. Name of Website. Web or Print (depending on format). Date
Retrieved.

Parts of Books

Just as short works are placed in quotation marks inside your essay,
they are similarly cited, as in the name of the article below: "Charles
Dickens's *A Tale of Two Cities* and the Power of the Everyday." I found
this article by running an Advanced search for an online, full-text journal article in the literature field with the title of Dickens' book as the
keyword. The title of the article, the journal, the date and the page
numbers were conveniently included in the heading of the page with
this article. The other components were also located on that first page,
with nothing hiding solely in the text of the article. In fact, the article
itself is in html, and it would have been harder to figure out the print
equivalent page number range from it.

The components in an article citation are more complex than for a
book. You have to remember to italicize the title of the journal and of
the database where the article is located, in addition to putting the title
of the article itself into quotations. Another component to remember
is including both the exact date when the issue was released and the
volume and issue number. Traditionally, journals were published in
loosely bound sections or issues, and then were all bound together at
the end of each year into a single volume. Today, most journals are per-
fect bound as individual issues, and only occasionally are they pulled
together into thick 400-plus page volumes by the libraries that collect
them. Many journals are released only digitally, so they are not even
released in print at all. Still the convention of organizing journals into
volumes and issues continues as it symbolically explains the flowing
nature of periodicals. If a work does not have a volume and issue des-
ignation, it is technically a stand-alone book and not a journal issue.
Some journals are basically a collection of books on specialty topics
(i.e.: Marxism, colonialism, abstraction, post-modernism, etc.) united
primarily by this numbering scheme and by a central editor. The Editor's name is not typically included in an article citation unless you are
citing the introduction or another unsigned portion that can only be
credited to the person tasked with pulling it all together.

Works Cited

Last Name, First. "Title of the Article." *Title of the Journal*, Volume Number (Issue Number), page number range. Publication Date. *Title of the Database*. Web or Print. Retrieval Date.

Lee, Klaudia. "Charles Dickens's *A Tale of Two Cities* and the Power of the Everyday." *The Explicator*, 74(1), pp. 5-7. 20 Mar 2016. *Taylor & Francis Online*. Web. 5 Nov 2016.

In-Text Citations

As I explained in the earlier section, some types of works should only be credited by title or creator's name in the text, instead of using a full in-text citation. One example of this exception is citing a quote from the lyrics of a music video. Typically, you do not need to include the minute or second where this segment begins. Even if you are quoting from a feature film, somebody who wants to duplicate your research, would typically watch the full film to find the quotes, or might grab a copy of the screenplay to search for this text. You still have to insert a full Works Cited entry for this work and explain where the quote comes from in your text.

When you are citing a quote from a digital ebook, typically you will not know which page number the quote is coming from in the original printed version of this book. Sometimes there might be line numbers or even page numbers include at the side of the html version of the book, and in these cases, you should take advantage of this information to make a full citation. But, if no page numbers are included, as in Gutenberg's *A Tale of Two Cities*, you should specify which chapter the quote is coming from to make it easier to locate. For example, in Chapter "XXIV. Drawn to the Loadstone Rock," Dickens' narrator exclaims:

> It was too much the way of Monseigneur under his reverses as a refugee, and it was much too much the way of native British orthodoxy, to talk of this terrible Revolution as if it were the only harvest ever known under the skies that had not been sown—as if nothing had ever been done, or omitted to be done, that had led to it—as if observers of the wretched millions in France, and of the misused and perverted resources that should have made them prosperous, had not seen it inevitably coming, years before, and had not in plain words recorded what they saw.

If there was a page number associated with this block quote, it would be inserted at the end of this long quotation. If you only want to insert a portion out of this long sentence, you might write that Dickens stresses that "observers of the wretched millions in France" saw "it inevitably coming, years before…" (Dickens "XXIV. Drawn to the Loadstone Rock," *Tale of Two Cities*). You should only insert the full name of the chapter and book title once in the sentences before a series of quotes or at the end of a string of quotes. If you begin citing a different source, you will want to repeat the citation to avoid confusion regarding where each bit of information is coming from.

To quote a portion out of the journal article, you should select the pdf version, which includes the page numbers missing from the html text. I grabbed the following quote connected to the theme of revolution: "Knitting in *A Tale of Two Cities* masks Madame Defarge's revolutionary activity because of its repetition and its everyday-ness; the air of normality that she puts up while carrying out this supposedly domestic act becomes a veil through which she observes her enemies" (Lee 5). I had to separate some words that ran into each other when I cut and pasted this text out of the article into this text. I also had to italicize the name of the book as italics do not transfer over in basic text insertions from online sources. At the end of the quote, I inserted the last name of the author of the article and the page number where this quote is from. You can see similar in-text citations if you find this or another scholarly article online that uses MLA citations. Other citation styles might include notes at the end of the article or at the end of the journal with the citations instead of including the page numbers right after the quotes. Even if you paraphrase text and do not include direct quotations, you have to include the page number or a page range (i.e.: (Lee 5-7)) at the end of the summary of what the article was about or a particular point from it.

Plagiarism and Academic Integrity

When the printing press was first invented, publishers in foreign countries on both sides of the Atlantic Ocean reproduced successful works from other publishers without paying them or their authors royalties because there were no clear copyrights laws. Later on, countries started granting licenses to be the sole printers of given works, but this did not deter thieves that worked underground or abroad. US only agreed to abide by the international copyrights treaty in 1989. Piracy of films, books as well as brand name clothing and various other goods is a major form of international crime to this day, with this black-market economy overwhelming international trade and causing billions in lost revenue to the companies that hold official copyrights and trademarks. The need to steal others' intellectual property in part stems from the corporatocracy that governs most "developed" capitalist countries. In a sea of competing businesses, a few giant corporations have broken into the mainstream and control enormous shares of the world markets in the products (including books and films) that they produce. Consumers want these high-status granting products because they have enormous marketing budgets that sell their apparent superior qualities. The prize on these commodities rises (Nike sneakers, Gucci bags) until poor people cannot afford them, but still crave them because of the marketing messages. So, in "developing" countries and among the poor in the "developed" world, people are happy to buy products that appear to be authentic, but are actually forged goods that closely mimic the originals. The producers of these goods might have otherwise created their own individual products, if they did so, they would have made significantly less because they would not be able to reach a global market with a marketing campaign to match the giant corporations. All this negative trade, seizures, imprisonments for piracy, and lost revenue are contributing to the world's current, decades-long Great Recession.

How does plagiarism in college classes fit into this global picture? *The Huffington Post* has posted articles reporting that 14% of Americans in 2013 could not read, or were illiterate. In one of my books, which you read a chapter out of earlier this semester, *Gender Bias in Mystery and Romance Novel Publishing*, I calculated that the grade level for mystery novels by women fell between 4.3 and 6.2. Romances novels written by men ranged between 4.7 and 7.6 reading levels. Mysteries by men were between 4.8 and 7.8 reading levels. Romances by women were between 2.5 and 6.8 reading levels. While some studies, such as the one by the National Center for Education Statistics, might have indicated that average Americans read at around an 8th grade level, the fact that best-selling novels across the past couple centuries always fall below this level suggests that this is an over-estimation. According to the "Bureau, U. C.: The 2009 Statistical Abstract: National Data Book," 85% of Americans have completed high school.

If all of the above statistics are correct, all of the illiterate Americans could not have completed high school, and of those who manage to complete high school, the reading level between them must be at an 8th or lower grade level despite the completion. So, they manage to pass classes in those last four years despite their reading and comprehension ability stopping at middle school... How can this be statistically possible? There is a black hole in the American education system. And a hypothesis I would like to propose is that this hole can be accounted for when plagiarism is brought into the equation. Only if students are purchasing essays or are otherwise fraudulently pumping up their grades can they manage to skate out of high school without learning anything over these four years.

Why should you avoid this black hole? Higher reading levels are associated with higher incomes, higher employment rates, longer lives and various other positive benefits. The ability to comprehend information and to express yourself is essential in the modern world. There are few jobs that do not require comprehension of some complex manuals, guides, reference sources, or law books. Anything from law enforcement to garbage truck operation requires knowledge of mechanical and human systems. If you do not understand and fail to look up key words in a required job manual, you can be headed for a catastrophic mechanical or personal failure. Better readers become leaders, while the bulk of the American prison population is illiterate. A free or a discounted state-sponsored education should not be squandered for an "easy" A. You will have to use your writing and communication ability for the rest of your life, and everybody you communicate with will plainly comprehend your actual reading/writing level, without going back to check on the grade you attained.

The term **academic integrity** means being honest and moral in the academic setting. The morality of academia is connected with the rights of the intellect (rather than property). Using somebody else's ideas as your own without giving proper credit to the source is called **plagiarism**. Nearly all schools, including UTRGV, have strict policies against plagiarism, and violations of intellectual property are punishable with course failure or even expulsion from a university. If students cheat on tests or purchase essays, they are artificially inflating the curve for the class, and this might drop the grades of the honest students.

This is why matters of academic dishonesty are treated very seriously and have strict sanctions. In addition, if you take content from Wikipedia, another student's essay, or from the web and insert it into your own essay, you are stealing their ideas and words. This theft can even be a criminal offense if you publish a plagiarized work online or in print, as at that point you are breaking another writer's legally guaranteed copyrights, and they can sue you for infringement.

There are a few rules to follow if you want to avoid plagiarism. Consulting encyclopedias and web sources is an important part of research writing. These steps are completed to fact-check your assumptions. It would be a logical error to record merely your assumptions or what you believe you know about a subject without first checking on these facts. Many writers misunderstand plagiarism and assume that if they give credit to the sources they consulted, it would be easier to prove that they plagiarized them. In truth, if you properly cite all of these sources, you will be properly completing the research assignment. A research paper should never be based solely on what you already know, but rather on what you learn from outside, well-cited sources. Because Wikipedia and some other un-checked web sources occasionally include mistakes, you should find reliable scholarly sources that you are not ashamed of properly crediting. Follow the same citation rules for most of these web sources as you would for articles out of an online journal. Even if you paraphrase information and do not use direct quotes, these citations are required. If you do use blocks of text from Wikipedia and do not credit Wikipedia, this is very likely to result in a 0 for the paper, or worse.

Works Cited

"Bureau, U. C.: The 2009 Statistical Abstract: National Data Book." *U. S. Census Bureau.* 2009. Web. 6 November 2016.

Faktorovich, Anna. *Gender Bias in Mystery and Romance Novel Publishing.* Augusta: Anaphora Literary Press, 2015.

Kirsch, Irwin S., Ann Jungeblut, Lynn Jenkins, and Andrew Kolstad. *Adult Literacy in America: A First Look at the Findings of the National Adult Literacy Survey. National Center for Education Statistics: U.S. Department of Education: Office of Educational Research and Improvement, Third Edition.* April 2002. Web. 6 November 2016.

"The U.S. Illiteracy Rate Hasn't Changed In 10 Years." *The Huffington Post.* 6 September 2013. Web. 6 November 2016.

Synthesis of Multiple Sources of Information

While a 2-page essay might only need one or two sources, you have to engage with a larger variety of sources in a 6-8+ page research paper. If you are citing from several sources, you have to be aware that the arguments in these sources might be contradictory or that they might not fit entirely into your central argument. Here are some hints on how to navigate potential problems that come in due to the complexity of source-integration into a research paper.

You have to keep track of your central argument across the writing process. Quoting or paraphrasing sources should not be done for its own sake, but rather to find evidence to support the central argument. Even if you insert an extra phrase in a quote that's irrelevant to your essay, it detracts from the argument by making an unnecessary digression.

For an example of how to integrate sources, let's jump back to the previous section, wherein I cited findings from the National Adult Literacy Survey. I should add that this survey seems to be a significant indicator because as National Center for Education Statistics' website claims, the "2003 National Assessment of Adult Literacy... NAAL is the nation's most comprehensive measure of adult literacy since the 1992 National Adult Literacy Survey (NALS)." While this seems to be a fair assessment, it is designed to make the picture seem less bleak than it actually is. For example, in a diagram summary in the "Demographics: Overall" section of the website, the researchers explain that 14% of American adults fall into the "below basic" level, whereas, if you'll recall, 14% of Americans are illiterate, so to call them "below basic" is inaccurate as they are at zero literacy rather than falling slightly below passing. The next level over is "basic," followed by "intermediate" and "proficient." Technically, everybody in the intermediate range also need remediation literacy classes, so that only 13% of Americans, in the "proficient" category is fully literate and able to comprehend written prose. If they had used a linguistic calculation for K-12 reading levels (as I did in my study of mystery and romance novels), it would have been easier to dissect the results, but instead they artificially defined these categories with alien classifications. With a significant portion of the US government's budget going towards education annually, these results are very negative in comparison with other developed countries.

As you can see, I have used quotes and data from a diagram to explain that I partially disagree with how these statistics are represented and calculated. I introduced the quotes with a hint of disagreement and then I explained what other relevant data adds to the argument. I cited the names of the articles in the Works Cited list below and within the text above. You should avoid merging more than two sources into a single paragraph to avoid making it too confusing for readers. You might want to discuss each new source in a separate paragraph, unless a couple of sources offer contradictory or parallel information and you have to compare or contrast them to explain the relationship between them. You always want to closely re-read the paragraphs where you are synthesizing information because any researcher is likely to slip up and fail to integrate the details fully with so much complex data and text in play.

If I examined another source for the argument about literacy above and it offered a contradictory argument supported by contradictory evidence, I would have used transition sentences and words to explain the relationship between them. I did this in part when I mentioned my own research into reading grade levels. I chose to refer to my study in parenthesis because it is a side note to the argument. If I was going to build further on this point to prove that the statistics from the NAAL study are inaccurate, I would have searched for additional secondary sources that supported my own findings, and would have included additional paragraphs or pages to strengthen this argument. Some of the best researched arguments aim to contradict previous findings or to show that somebody else's research was insufficient or otherwise erroneous. If you plan on arguing with a government agency, like the NAAL, you will face some difficulty because they report that they sampled thousands of people in their studies, so duplicating their experiment or attempting to create a better one would be extremely costly, considering the expense of finding, querying, calculating the statistics and otherwise pulling together an equivalent study. In my study, I looked at a couple dozen novels, and it is easy to ridicule this by asking why I did not look at thousands of novels to make sure that my reading level statistics were exact for all best-selling fiction. Without government funding, it is extremely difficult for any sole researcher to challenge earlier government findings. So, as a beginner researcher, try to avoid statistics and work on making arguments based on quotations and narratives from individual books or films.

Works Cited

"What is NAAL?" *National Assessment of Adult Literacy: National Center for Education Statistics.* Web. 6 November 2016.

"Demographics: Overall." *National Assessment of Adult Literacy: National Center for Education Statistics.* Web. 6 November 2016.

Part 8

The Research Paper

This part begins with the Research Paper Assignment. Then, information is provided to assist students with inventing ideas that might be suitable for this larger research project. They are also taught how to narrow their topic to avoid digressing into unrelated topics or picking a topic that's too broad to be covered fully in a relatively short research paper. And they are instructed on the best way to organize any research paper.

Research Paper Assignment

Write an 8-page research paper on a fictional book or fictitious feature film through the lens of one of the central cultural concepts we studied this semester: gender, ethnicity or ideology. You should not duplicate one of your previous short essays, but you can base this essay on the same artifact you chose previously if it fits the requirements for this essay. If you base this essay on an earlier essay, you should not borrow such a large quantity of exact content that you might be flagged for plagiarism by SafeAssign. Ideally, you should write about a new artifact, as you need at least four secondary sources in addition to your primary artifact. There might not be enough of these on your earlier idea. Because there has been a lot of confusion regarding what constitutes an "artifact," for this research paper, only fictional books and films are suitable. Thus, do *not* write this essay about non-fiction biographies or about cultural artifacts such as the burka. The narrative component of the assignment specifies that you have to narrate the plot depicted in the artifact, so these ideas cannot meet the spirit of this component. The use of secondary sources is essential for a research paper. Some of you have not been utilizing any secondary sources in the short essays. It is improbably that an 8-page research paper can be written without the use of at least four secondary sources, so for this essay their use, proper citation and integration counts as 20% of the paper.

In addition to 10% of this essay being based on your participation in the Editing Workshop, another 10% will be based on your 3-minute presentation of your research findings. You will be expected to talk for the full 3-minutes duration. If you choose to read a short version of your paper, it should be a coherent summary that fits in the 3-minute window. Ideally, you should be familiar enough with your research to talk about it for these 3 minutes without reading. You might want to create notecards to remind you of your key points. We will spend the entire class on this project. If some students are absent or choose not to participate and receive a 0 for this component, the leftover time will be used to ask your fellow students questions about their research.

Here is the breakdown of the components of this research paper:

- the presence of a narrative of the plotline or story depicted in the artifact (10%)
- the proper use, citation and integration of at least four second-

ary, scholarly sources (preferably found through the UTRGV Library website) related to the artifact or the concept (20%)
- a central cohesive argument (10%)
- relate a film/book to one of the central concepts discussed this semester: gender, ethnicity or ideology (10%)
- a clear writing style that is readable and lacks major errors (30%)
- 3-minute presentation of your research findings to the class (10%)
- participation in the Editing Workshop (10%)

Strategies for Idea Invention

Invention of new technologies or medical cures can take decades if not centuries. As a result, the thought of inventing a new idea for an essay might appear to be daunting. But research papers in the humanities and social sciences are unlike scientific breakthroughs. Even dissertations or books on humanities subjects are seldom complete separations from earlier studies. New research relies on earlier findings and there is no patent process to go through before research can be released to the reading public. Occasionally, the stakes are just as high when politics or economics of a nation are at stake. But, when you are writing an essay for a college class rather than for publication, your audience is small and the primary challenge is finding a way to interest yourself in your research topic. If you can find an idea you are curious to learn more about, reading secondary sources on the subject will be enjoyable, educational and fleeing. If you have to write about any book or film, you should begin by choosing something that fits the assignment and that's a favorite of yours. Once you have picked a field of study, and if you are familiar with some of the ideas discussed in this part of the book, the rest of the essay should flow naturally without the need for you to re-invent a wheel.

If the assignment is to research a book or a film, once you choose it, this is your primary source of inspiration. The plotline, characters, descriptions, and other elements should suggest the key points you have to make to support your argument. On the other hand, if you do not have a favorite film or book, you can instead begin by finding a concept that you are interested in. Perhaps, you are already curious about gender bias or affirmative action, but if you have not researched these subjects previously, you might consider searching for inspiration by listening to news reports, or watching comedies about the world around you, or reading general, introductory books about the field you are asked to focus on. As you read, view, or browse through these materials, ideas might pop into your mind in response.

If an essay assignment does not specify a field of study, you might find inspiration from your casual conversations with the people around you. You might need to think back over the conversations you have had in the last few years, rather than this past week. If you have had passionate discussions about a political or social topic, you are likely to be excited about researching it.

Finally, keep in mind, inspiration does not come to those who wait.

Don't procrastinate. At the stage when you are unsure which artifact or concept interests you, just start writing whatever comes to mind when you think about the assignment. A list of possible films or books might be running through your mind, and if you write a sentence on which each of these would work or fail to come together will help you to choose the best out of these options. If you figure out which ideas do not work with a sentence, this is more efficient than if you discover this after you have written the bulk of the essay. Jotting down ideas is also necessary for narrowing or widening the topic, as explained in the next section.

Narrowing the Topic

There are a few general rules to follow regardless of the type of essay you are writing. First, all research papers are also arguments, which need to convince the reader of the veracity, morality, applicability or the like of your thesis or proposal. This means that there has to be somebody on the planet that disagrees with your argument or has objected to it. For example, if you choose to write a paper that asserts that people breathe, it is unlikely you will find anybody that would contest this long-proven fact. So, you would really be summarizing a fact and the evidence that has long supported this fact. A summary is a narration rather than an argument, and therefore this would not be a good research paper. Arguments that have potential opposing points of view or at least two sides are called debatable arguments. In addition, do your best to choose a side in the debate. Avoid writing "maybe" papers. Rephrase or refocus your thesis into one that you are sure about. If your argument is extremely balanced between the opposing sides and you waver between them, the reader will have a sense that you failed to decide on a position. Indecision looks like incompletion or a failure to figure the issue out thoroughly before digesting it clearly for your readers in the essay.

Another way of narrowing the scope of your essay is to focus on a topic that fits the length of the assignment. A 2-page essay should be narrower in focus than an 8-page essay or a book-length research study. I have noticed this in a lot of your essays. Many of you choose topics, such as fascism in general, or present a general argument about a dense book, and then try to condense a whole field of study into a 2-page paper. The mini-research paper assignments are designed for you to learn how to insert just the necessary quantity of quotes and paraphrases from secondary sources to sustain your argument in the few words available to you. While the assignments asked you to touch on gender studies, ethnicity and ideology, I have presented many sub-categories of these including topics such as linguistics and capitalism. These sub-categories are still too broad for a 2-page essay. If they were narrow-enough, there would not be enough possible topics to allow all of the students to come up with their own sub-fields to focus on. Within capitalism, monopolies might also be too broad, so that you should specify the country, region, or a specific monopoly you are examining. Generalizing about all people in a gender, an ethnicity or about all monopolies is likely to be a logical fallacy unless you have solid proof to support this conclusion.

Of course, for a research paper one of the most important factors that should limit the scope of your essay is the availability of relevant secondary sources on the concept or artifact of your choosing. You should begin with a search for sources through the Library's website on key terms related to your topic. If you cannot find the required quantity of sources, you should change the artifact or the concept, or you should broaden or narrow the subject to something that you can find enough sources on.

To avoid digressing into unrelated topics, it's a good idea to start the essay by writing your central thesis in the first sentence. For the Research Paper, this thesis should include the name of the fictional film or book you are researching and one of the concepts in gender, ethnicity or ideology studies that we have reviewed. Basically, the thesis is a sentence with your topic as the subject and what you plan on doing with it as the verb phrase (though frequently the explanation is not an actual verb).

You also want to narrow the topic geographically, in its time period, and by other measures. Zoom into a region, such as the South versus the North in the United States, or another segment of the population, so that you can find clear quantitative (i.e. statistics) or qualitative (i.e. value judgment) evidence to support your narrow argument. Generalizations about all people all over the world are unlikely to be truthful. In other words, if you say that all men or women everywhere are X or Y, this statement is unlikely to be true, even if you insert *breathe* and *eat* in for X and Y. Some people might be on a hunger strike and others might be temporarily failing to breathe at the time your essay was written, thus your assertion would be inaccurate. On the other hand, if you specify the ethnicity, region, economic group, and other indicators in the group that show a pattern and then make your statement, it is more likely that your assertion will be factual.

Once you choose a narrow topic, and now need to explore your topic for sub-points to discuss. You can try asking yourself some relevant questions that might start with *who, what, when, where, why* and *how* about the connection between your artifact and concept, and jot down your replies. This brainstorming exercise might help you come up with an innovative idea for your research paper that was not apparent before you questioned yourself.

One of the questions you might want to ask yourself is: *What is the nature of the artifact I am examining?* This can lead you in many different directions, including identifying the genre it belongs to, such as if it is a comedy, romance, tragedy, mystery, or experimental. You might also think about if it propagandizes for something or if it is clearly intended to be pure entertainment without a heavier moral or political message. Even pure entertainment caries a heavy cultural message. Anarchy, over-indulgence in mind-altering drugs, and sexual promiscuity are topics that are heavily debated in the media and political arenas. When you think about the nature of your artifact for this essay, you should think about the nature of your chosen concept (gender, ethnicity, ideology) in the borders of this work.

Another question you might want to ask is: *What can this artifact be compared or contrasted to that might explain its nature better?* Is this film or book very different from the other artifacts in the genre that it is placed into? For example, many of you wrote about the 2006 comedy, *She's the Man*, for the gender essay. In this film, a girl disguises herself as her brother and plays soccer successfully in his place. In theory, this film is doing something positive by portraying a girl that has the freedom to cross-dress, but it is also saying that she has to cross-dress to be respected because girls are not accepted as naturally good soccer players. The argument that this film is making a positive, empowering message can be strengthened by comparing it to other comedies about cross-dressing and checking if there is a message they have in common or if there are some that are more respectful of gender fluidity. If you plan on generalizing about all films in the genre to say, for example, that the heroines are typically portrayed as being thin, beautiful and timid, you have to name a few of the films you are thinking about that lead you to this generalization. Though, even if you can name a few of these, you should avoid saying that all films portray anything in the same way because there are always some outliers in any genre.

A more difficult question to ask is: *Why is this concept portrayed in this way in so many artifacts in a given culture and genre?* Cultural norms are not spontaneous. Similarly to a political campaign, somebody has to actively lobby to portray women as the weaker or less intelligent sex. The responsible party might be an owner of a film production company or it might be the majority of pro-patriarchal males in a culture. If you think about who benefits from an aspect of our cultural biases, you might be moving towards the truth of the matter.

Another question to ask is: *What do secondary sources say about the components of my research project?* You should ask this question as early as possible after you begin the paper. If you consult sources after you write the bulk of your own argument, you might discover that authorities in the field you are researching disagree with your findings. Then, you will have to prove them all wrong, or you will have to discard all of your earlier writing and start the paper from the beginning to fit with these contradictory ideas. Usually, you will find some scholars that agree with you and others that disagree. If they all fall on a single side, this is probably not a good topic to write about as all good arguments have at least two sides to them. If the scholars disagree, you have to figure out where your views lie in this debate.

Organizing a Research Paper

Each individual has their own preferences for essay organization strategies. Some writers do not do any preparation before simply sitting down and writing the research paper from start to finish, as they read the sources and craft the argument around these. Other writers need to write a detailed outline to figure out what their supporting points will be before they start dissecting the sources. For the essays assigned in this class, it's a good idea to begin by reading or viewing your primary source, and then read the secondary sources. As you read, take careful notes with quotes and paraphrasing. Even if it seems that you will recall what the article was about a day or a week after reading it, you should not take a chance, and instead record the summary right after you finish the whole article or perhaps a key paragraph that is particularly relevant. If you do this correctly, you should have a list of quotes and some paraphrases of the important relevant bits from the primary and secondary sources organized by the name of the source. Remember to insert proper in-text and Works Cited page citations for all of these quotes and paraphrases because it is unlikely you will recall which page number each of them came from later on.

Once the evidence is in front of you, organize these quotes and ideas into groups that might fall into paragraphs or parts of the paper. You can separate them into what should come in the beginning, or information that introduces the concept in a noticeable or interesting way, and then what would below in the middle (body) and the end (conclusion). Alternatively, you would write the introduction and conclusion after you write the body, so instead you would separate the evidence into sub-points that the different bits of evidence are proving. If you fail to group ideas together into categories, readers will notice this because your ideas will jump around disconnectedly.

If you are writing a long research paper, in addition to separating information into categories you will want to create an outline around it to tell you which points you want to make about each of the groupings. The outline should have an introduction, conclusion, and body paragraphs that focus on your key points. This outline does not have to be written in a traditional style. If you gathered quotes and paraphrasing as noted above, your outline can be phrases or sentences inserted at the start of each of your parts. Alternatively, you might want to put in bold the key words or points in each of the bits of information that you are grouping together. This way, when you scan these groups and notice primarily the bold words, you will understand better the overall point you are making and the relationship between the bolded points. After you finish this phase, you would then start actually writing the explanations that will make the quotes and paraphrases clear to your reader. Your own argument should fit in between these bits of evidence. For example, as you are reading or viewing your artifact, you might write the narration of what happens in its plot. Then you can put in bold the key elements in this plot that are pertinent to your central research. And when you go back to insert your argument into or after this narration, you can stress and explain these key bits of relevant proof.

You might also find that some of the evidence uncovered during the note-taking stage is irrelevant to your central argument. Do not be afraid to take out these irrelevant bits. A strong researched argument cannot include digressions into irrelevant content simply because you also noticed it during your research.

Writing Exercise

Write a brief newspaper-style opinion story paragraph about the artifact you are thinking of writing the research paper about. Answer these questions: *who, what, when, where, why* and *how*. In particular focus on the following detailed questions:

What is the nature of the artifact I am examining?

What can this artifact be compared or contrasted to that might explain its nature better? Give examples.

Why is this concept portrayed in this way in so many artifacts in a given culture and genre?

Discuss your fellow students' replies.

Part 9

Grabbing Attention

Introductions and Conclusions

The final part attempts to inspire students with how they can grab the reader's attention with catch Introductions and Conclusions. In the last weeks of class, it might be a good idea for students to do presentations on what they have learned through writing the research paper.

Some of you have been writing very theoretical and reflective introductory paragraphs. I have been critical of this because frequently you include information that is not fully relevant to the narrow topic you might hope to cover in a 2-page paper. On the other hand, many of these reflections have been very insightful, and I would rather not discourage a good thing. So, in this section, I am going to write a bit about some of the ways you might try to grab the reader's attention. Ideally, you should still introduce the concept and artifact you are covering in the very first sentence, but once you have oriented your reader on your topic, there is some room for creative nonfiction.

The best way to learn how to write is by reading. Three excerpts are included below that are connected with ethnicity, gender and ideology. They introduce the concepts that the rest of these books elaborate on in a way that grabs the reader's attention and welcomes them in.

The first example is from Booker T. Washington's *Up from Slavery: An Autobiography*.

> Of my ancestry I know almost nothing. In the slave quarters, and even later, I heard whispered conversations among the coloured people of the tortures which the slaves, including, no doubt, my ancestors on my mother's side, suffered in the middle passage of the slave ship while being conveyed from Africa to America. I have been unsuccessful in securing any information that would throw any accurate light upon the history of my family beyond my mother. She, I remember, had a half-brother and a half-sister. In the days of slavery not very much attention was given to family history and

family records—that is, black family records. My mother, I suppose, attracted the attention of a purchaser who was afterward my owner and hers. Her addition to the slave family attracted about as much attention as the purchase of a new horse or cow. Of my father I know even less than of my mother. I do not even know his name. I have heard reports to the effect that he was a white man who lived on one of the near-by plantations. Whoever he was, I never heard of his taking the least interest in me or providing in any way for my rearing. But I do not find especial fault with him. He was simply another unfortunate victim of the institution which the Nation unhappily had engrafted upon it at that time (Washington "Chapter I. A Slave Among Slaves").

While appealing to emotions is a logical fallacy that tries to convince by hitting the reader's sense of pity or sympathy with the pains suffered by slaves, this is one of the more positive examples of this manipulation. Some readers need to have their emotions stirred to enter a narrative, as they are repelled by pure logic. You should not be using the first person "I" in your research papers, nor should you be narrating stories from your own life. But this is a great example of a narrative summary that only covers the parts that are relative to the primary purpose of the book. Washington is writing about his life to demonstrate the difficulties African Americans had as slaves and then as freedmen. So, this summary begins in the slave ships and stresses that there was so little value to slaves' lives that he could find little concrete evidence about his heritage. Ethnicity is primarily associated with extended relatives and ties to an ancient past, but with no records of this extended family tree and with their traditions wiped out in the enslavement process, Washington struggles with an emptiness where a sense of this extended self should be. He also uses metaphors, such as equating slaves to horses and cows to intensify the powerlessness his family felt in these circumstances. Metaphors, symbolism and other figurative language frequently helps to draw an emotional parallel where the facts fail to convey the depth of the problem. The discussion about his father is another key detail related to ethnicity and the identity of mixed black-and-white children such as Washington. He does not digress into the story of who told him the gossip about his father or what they said, but rather focuses on his whiteness and the problem of how the system desensitized him with racism to the point that he did not feel any filial attraction towards his son. There are no irrelevant bits of information, or overlong wails about his lot. All of the words are essential to making the main point and convincing readers in his thesis.

One of my favorite non-fiction books is Virginia Woolf's *A Room of*

One's Own.

But, you may say, we asked you to speak about women and fiction—what, has that got to do with a room of one's own? I will try to explain. When you asked me to speak about women and fiction I sat down on the banks of a river and began to wonder what the words meant... The title women and fiction might mean, and you may have meant it to mean, women and what they are like, or it might mean women and the fiction that they write; or it might mean women and the fiction that is written about them, or it might mean that somehow all three are inextricably mixed together and you want me to consider them in that light. But when I began to consider the subject in this last way, which seemed the most interesting, I soon saw that it had one fatal drawback. I should never be able to come to a conclusion. I should never be able to fulfil what is, I understand, the first duty of a lecturer to hand you after an hour's discourse a nugget of pure truth to wrap up between the pages of your notebooks and keep on the mantelpiece for ever. All I could do was to offer you an opinion upon one minor point—a woman must have money and a room of her own if she is to write fiction; and that, as you will see, leaves the great problem of the true nature of woman and the true nature of fiction unsolved. I have shirked the duty of coming to a conclusion upon these two questions—women and fiction remain, so far as I am concerned, unsolved problems. But in order to make some amends I am going to do what I can to show you how I arrived at this opinion about the room and the money... At any rate, when a subject is highly controversial—and any question about sex is that—one cannot hope to tell the truth. One can only show how one came to hold whatever opinion one does hold. One can only give one's audience the chance of drawing their own conclusions as they observe the limitations, the prejudices, the idiosyncrasies of the speaker. Fiction here is likely to contain more truth than fact. Therefore I propose, making use of all the liberties and licences of a novelist, to tell you the story of the two days that preceded my coming here—how, bowed down by the weight of the subject which you have laid upon my shoulders, I pondered it, and made it work in and out of my daily life. I need not say that what I am about to describe has no existence; Oxbridge is an invention; so is Fernham; 'I' is only a convenient term for somebody who has no real being. Lies will flow from my lips, but there may perhaps be some truth mixed up with them; it is for you to seek out this truth and to decide whether any part of it is worth keeping. If not, you will of course throw the whole of it into the waste-paper basket and forget all about it (Woolf "One").

There are many points raised above that pertain to both the process of writing and the topic of gender bias. There are many college courses, textbooks, artbooks and other artifacts that include the word "women" in their titles. Women are frequently grouped together or only a single woman might be inserted into a book dedicated to high-achieving men for the sake of tokenism. This book began as a speech Woolf gave to a college class. Like all great writers, Woolf dared to diverge from the typical lectures she must have heard or read on "women and fiction." Similarly, you should feel encouraged to object to the opinions and theories of the scholars you read in your secondary sources. Simply because most of the people writing about "women and fiction" were men, Woolf had an entirely unique perspective on the problem as a successful female author and publisher of her own Hogarth Press. Woolf wrote this piece over a decade after she started the press with her husband, Leonard, and yet she hardly mentions the venture in this long essay. Woolf sets out to prove that her failures to become a bestseller or to see more success in her press or with her teaching are due to her gender, and for her it all boils down simply to money, which she symbolically represents with a "room" that she wishes she had to herself. She moved from her family's home to a place with her husband and hardly spent a night in a room of her own across her relatively short life. She committed suicide in 1941 in part out of depression over the state of things for her as a woman, and in part out of fear that the Nazis might invade her region and might put her and her Jewish husband into a concentration camp. This book shows the intensity of Woolf's emotions on the topic of gender bias in fiction, her chosen vocation. She is famous for her stream-of-consciousness writing style, wherein she writes long sentences that jump from one idea to the next as they occur to her. This type of flighty reflection is generally frivolous and should be avoided in research papers, but this excerpt is an example of it at its best. Numerous ideas are condensed into this paragraph. Woolf even talks about the difference between fiction and non-fiction. She proves and explains the difference with pure deductive logic, without unnecessary examples to support her points. If you read the text closely, you will notice how she weaves the ideas together to arrive at each piece in the chain. Most of the arguments I have noticed in your papers attempt this type of pure logic, but you jump from A to L or from C to Z without working through the bits that if left unexplored become presumptions or logical fallacies. If you are going to jump between points, you have to use more concrete evidence, such as a respected scholars' quotes or statistics, as proof. Even if you do not want to attempt this complex argumentative style, this quote should help any of you who are writing the research paper on gender.

The last quote also comes from a book that I started admiring early on in my own studies, Henry David Thoreau's *Walden*. Thoreau makes an argument in defense of the two years he spent living of the land in a house he built himself by the Walden pond. He explains in an earlier paragraph that he is making a defense against direct ridicule and inquisitions he heard from his neighbors that objected to his way of life. Thoreau attempts to prove that isolation, hard toil and withdrawing from the capitalist economy are essential to attaining happiness.

> I see young men, my townsmen, whose misfortune it is to have inherited farms, houses, barns, cattle, and farming tools; for these are more easily acquired than got rid of. Better if they had been born in the open pasture and suckled by a wolf, that they might have seen with clearer eyes what field they were called to labor in. Who made them serfs of the soil? Why should they eat their sixty acres, when man is condemned to eat only his peck of dirt? Why should they begin digging their graves as soon as they are born? They have got to live a man's life, pushing all these things before them, and get on as well as they can. How many a poor immortal soul have I met well-nigh crushed and smothered under its load, creeping down the road of life, pushing before it a barn seventy-five feet by forty, its Augean stables never cleansed, and one hundred acres of land, tillage, mowing, pasture, and woodlot! The portionless, who struggle with no such unnecessary inherited encumbrances, find it labor enough to subdue and cultivate a few cubic feet of flesh (Thoreau "Economy").

In truth, Thoreau's mother gave him the piece of land by the pond, so he might be among the "young men" that had the "misfortune" to inherit a farm. Thoreau does not dwell on this glitch though, but instead stresses that people who engage in farming or factory work are equally enslaved by the capitalist system that works them to death without fair compensation. The "soul" is crushed under this labor, and Thoreau pleas that the soul should be protected. Just enough labor should be exerted to survive rather than toiling beyond the breaking point. The techniques Thoreau is using here are exaggeration, metaphors, questioning, and appeal to the reader's feelings about and practical aversion to labor. The trick in the first sentence in this paragraph is especially well done. Thoreau reverses the common cliché that an inheritance is desired by all, and instead points out that it is a misfortune. He then proves this controversial assertion by using a metaphor of the wolves being freer than a working man. Then, he asks the reader questions about labor, land, life and death to place the reader into his perspective rather than leaving them isolated in thinking that they are the "young men" of inheritance that Thoreau is ridiculing. From there, he uses specific, descriptive language to bring the image of labor on the soil into the reader's mind so that an abstract idea is colored with facts and details.

These three examples of great argumentative writing are overflowing with lessons for anybody from a beginner writer to a scholar, and they are cited by both in fitting quantities. If you are ever unsure about how you should begin or end a paper, read these or other wise excerpts for inspiration.

Works Cited

Thoreau, Henry David. *Walden, and On the Duty of Civil Disobedience.* (1854). January 1995. Web. 25 November 2016.

Washington, Booker T. *Up from Slavery: An Autobiography.* (1901). Project Gutenberg. 20 October 2008. Web. 25 November 2016.

Woolf, Virginia. *A Room of One's Own.* (1929). Project Gutenberg of Australia eBook. October 2002. Web. 25 November 2016.

OTHER ANAPHORA LITERARY PRESS TITLES

The History of British and American Author-Publishers
By: Anna Faktorovich

Notes for Further Research
By: Molly Kirschner

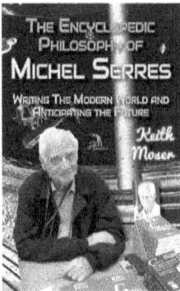

The Encyclopedic Philosophy of Michel Serres
By: Keith Moser

The Visit
By: Michael G. Casey

How to Be Happy
By: C. J. Jos

A Dying Breed
By: Scott Duff

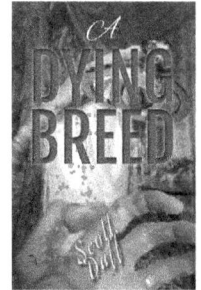

Love in the Cretaceous
By: Howard W. Robertson

The Second of Seven
By: Jeremie Guy

www.ingramcontent.com/pod-product-compliance
Lightning Source LLC
Chambersburg PA
CBHW020921090426
42736CB00008B/741